Warwickshire Landscapes
The Story So Far

Dedicated to Marian, Clare and Lucy

First published 2009

Published by Shay Books
2 Belmont Drive
Leamington Spa, CV32 6LS
www.shaybooks.co.uk
01926· 337195
© **Michael Jeffs, 2009**

ISBN: 978-0-9562773-0-5

Printed in Great Britain by the MPG Books Group,
Bodmin and Kings Lynn

Front cover photos: Harvest scene, Polesworth Abbey, Hatton Locks,
View from Edge Hill

CONTENTS

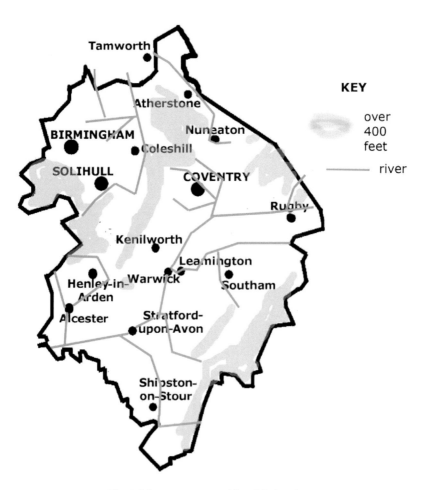

KEY

over 400 feet

—— river

Fig 1. The area covered by this book

Introduction

Summary and Aims of the Book, What is Warwickshire?

This book examines the landscapes of Warwickshire to see what they look like now and how they came to be this way. The aim is to gain some idea of what the landscape was like at different times in history and to describe the factors which have affected the landscapes which we see today. The book considers and discusses some of the social, industrial, agricultural, geological and other influences which have shaped the landscape throughout many millions of years.

The book does not claim to provide a full history of the county or to give the history of all of its famous people. It cannot give the history of every settlement but a number of examples are mentioned in various centuries such as Nuneaton, Coleshill, Kenilworth, Coventry, Kineton, Leamington Spa, Long Compton, Warwick and Alcester amongst others. The repeated references to the growth of various villages, towns and cities are intentional and highlight the sequence of marks left on the landscape by the works of man as the population grew and fluctuated and lifestyles changed.

Suggestions are made in Appendix 2 about areas of the county for exploration where the results of these influences can be seen and experienced. The book points out landscape features, buildings and other evidence of the past which has survived into the present. It cannot give a detailed history of the landscape at every site in the county but it is hoped to give some clues about how you can observe an area and imagine how it has changed over time.

What is Warwickshire?

A key preliminary consideration is what is meant by Warwickshire. The current political boundaries are largely a construction of the 1970s. In considering the history of the area this book includes the geographical areas of Birmingham, Coventry and Solihull which, of course, did not exist for a number of the early chapters of the book. Over the centuries various parishes were transferred to and taken from the ancient administrative county of Warwickshire by Worcestershire, Gloucestershire, Northamptonshire, Oxfordshire and Staffordshire (see Fig 2). The boundaries in earlier years have therefore been treated as somewhat flexible.

Therefore the boundaries of Warwickshire have not been constant over the centuries. For example Coventry became a separate county in 1451 and Birmingham became a county much later in 1888. Solihull became a county borough in 1965 and the Meriden Gap became part of the West Midlands in 1974. The situation in the south was more complex. In 1844 one detached parish moved from the county to Worcestershire and another moved in 1931. One parish each was moved from Northamptonshire and Oxfordshire in 1895. Eleven parishes including Shipston-on-Stour were allocated to Warwickshire from Worcestershire and three from Gloucestershire in 1931. In the north the town of Tamworth was within Warwickshire from the first naming of the county in about 1001 until 1888. The present-day administrative county of Warwickshire includes 220 parish, district and borough councils. In addition there are Solihull town plus 12 parish councils in Solihull Borough Council. However there are no parish councils in Nuneaton and Bedworth, Coventry and Birmingham. This has resulted in a total of 235 administrative units in the historical area of Warwickshire.

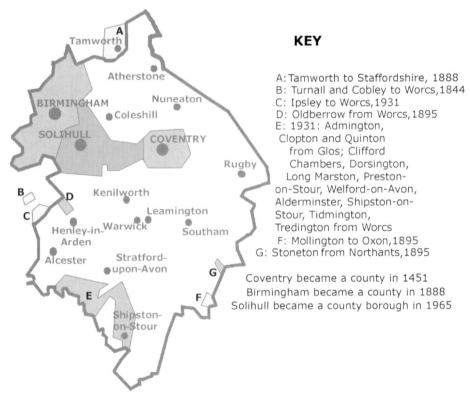

KEY

A: Tamworth to Staffordshire, 1888
B: Turnall and Cobley to Worcs, 1844
C: Ipsley to Worcs, 1931
D: Oldberrow from Worcs, 1895
E: 1931: Admington,
    Clopton and Quinton
    from Glos; Clifford
    Chambers, Dorsington,
    Long Marston, Preston-
    on-Stour, Welford-on-Avon,
    Alderminster, Shipston-on-
    Stour, Tidmington,
    Tredington from Worcs
F: Mollington to Oxon, 1895
G: Stoneton from Northants, 1895

Coventry became a county in 1451
Birmingham became a county in 1888
Solihull became a county borough in 1965

Fig 2. Map showing the boundary changes

To add some context Warwickshire adjoins Worcestershire which is the inspiration for the fictional Ambridge, the home of the Archers. It is also worth noting that Warwickshire is as far from the sea as you can get in Britain and it is surrounded by seven counties. There are two sites at Leamington Spa and Meriden which are reputed to be the centre of England.

Impact of Man on the Landscapes

The impact of man on the countryside comes from four main sources: agriculture, settlement, transport and industry.

After the major geological changes finished with the retreat of the ice sheets between 10,000 and 12,000 BC the landscape has been fashioned by nature and the people together. The land was first colonised by plant life and this was then followed by animals and mankind. Animals including men used the plant and animal life for food and man also used trees and shrubs and the landscape for shelter.

Fig 3. A view which combines the magic ingredients of land, trees and water. The River Avon at Bubbenhall

People were initially hunter-gatherers but gradually realised that it could be less energetic and more productive and efficient to cultivate some plants and to rear animals. This began to shape the landscape. It is impossible to tell with any certainty how significant the impact on the landscape was at different times in early history since very little evidence remains. It has largely been erased by later use of the land by man. At first men probably lived in family or tribal groups and were largely nomadic. At some time these groups found it possible to settle in a vicinity for a length of time. This was probably seasonal so there may have been a winter and a summer camp.

It is impossible to know what influenced the groups to stay or to move or what influenced their choice of sites. There may have been religious beliefs as well as the practical issues around ease of finding food, water, fire and shelter. We do not know whether groups lived in peace or whether there were frequent battles. However buried bodies found with injuries of battle and sites of forts have been found which indicate some war-like activity.

Acknowledgements

I would like to take an early opportunity to thank the many authors of the works on paper and the web which were referred to in my research. The main sources are listed in Appendix 1. I am particularly fond of the wide range of works written by LTC (Tom) Rolt. I am also grateful to Susan Wallbank for her assistance in many ways and to Giles Carey of the Warwickshire County Council Museum Service for help with sourcing photographs. I would also like to thank my wife, Marian, for her patience and support.

A proportion of the net proceeds from the sale of this book will be donated to the Warwickshire Branch of the Campaign to Protect Rural England (CPRE) and WaterAid.

For the curious, the name of the publisher, Shay Books, is taken from a type of geared steam locomotive once common on the logging lines of North America. They are another interest of the author.

Michael Jeffs, Royal Leamington Spa, July 2009

Chapter One

Geology

Overview, Continental Drift

At first glance the countryside of today appears to be timeless and unchanging. But this is far from the truth. Many huge changes have taken place in the landscapes of Warwickshire over millions of years. This chapter will explore the main changes in our countryside before man appeared on the scene. Many of us find the geological past, looking back over an immense time of 4,500 million years, difficult to comprehend. The reference to geological time periods and hundreds of millions of years can be daunting but it is hoped that the 'Timeline' panel at the end of this chapter will help to clarify matters.

In this chapter the abbreviation Ma is used to represent the phrase 'million years ago'.

It may be hard to imagine, but over hundreds of millions of years the surface of Warwickshire has been created by deep seas, river deltas, volcanoes, swamps, shallow warm tropical seas and deep frozen glaciers - a far cry from today's rolling agricultural landscapes with a temperate climate. These changes put our current debates about climate changes into a wider context. The current time is sometimes referred to as an inter-glacial period.

A major early factor is that Continental Drift has caused England and Wales to move generally northwards across the surface of the Earth, typically at a rate of about 4 centimetres (1.5 inches) per year. This would amount to about 4,000 kilometres in 100 million years. Around 500 Ma (in the Cambrian Period), when primitive life was forming in the seas, the entire land mass of England was situated near the South Pole. England, Wales, Southern Ireland, and a small part of NE America formed a drifting subcontinent known as Avalonia. By 350 million years ago in the Carboniferous Period England had joined up to Scotland which was part of another land mass which had travelled from the west. The Scottish Highlands were created by the continental collision of these two land masses. At the time that this collision occurred Britain was situated near the equator.

That is a brief geological history of Britain. We will see that the geology of Warwickshire falls very crudely into two zones. To the north and west is the

11

area broadly known as Arden and to the south and east is Feldon. The boundary is roughly along the valley of the River Avon. Both areas have a complex geological history. There are also other named areas on the fringes. These are described in more detail in Appendix 3.

Fig 4. A view from the limestone hills of the Cotswolds at Ilmington Hill looking south-east across the Fosse Way towards Shipston-on-Stour.
This hill is at the northern extremity of the Cotswolds and it is well protected as part of the Cotswolds Area of Outstanding Natural Beauty.

The Ice Ages

At various times between 400,000 and roughly 12,000 to 10,000 years ago the whole area of the county was covered by ice sheets. The ice sometimes stretched across the whole of Britain and into northern France but it is believed that the last Ice Age ended north of the Thames Valley. When this ice melted large amounts of glacial deposits were dumped, particularly on and around Dunsmore Heath. Many Warwickshire villages are located on top of these deposits as they give easy access to sub-surface water.

The science of geology can be crudely split into two areas. The first deals with the underlying rocks which are not too far from the surface; the study of these is generally known as Bedrock or Solid geology. Then there is the study of the material, mainly soil, which lies on the surface; this is referred to as Drift geology. Both these components of the land surface can have complex histories.

The impact of geology is apparent in the formation and use of the surface of the land. It is also the basis for quarrying and mining which leave their present-day marks on the countryside both in terms of the quarries, pits, mines and spoil heaps themselves but also the homes and industrial works that were established nearby.

Fig 5. Corley Rocks, a rare outcrop of sandstone in the county

Arden - Precambrian, Cambrian and Ordovician (4500 Ma to 450 Ma)

The oldest rocks of the Precambrian, Cambrian and Ordovician periods in Warwickshire are confined to the north where huge quarries have been dug to exploit them for aggregate for road foundations. Rocks of these types are found only along the narrow Nuneaton Ridge which runs between Nuneaton and Atherstone. These are very old rocks indeed and date from 615 Ma – 500 Ma. They were formed when a large pocket of quartzite was forced to the surface by volcanic action and this material is quarried at Hartshill near Nuneaton. These ancient rocks originated as sheets of molten material injected under pressure into earlier rocks as layers of ash were thrown out of volcanoes to fall into the surrounding ocean. Today, the rocks are amongst the toughest to be found in the county. Hartshill has a large variety of rocks including volcanic tuffs, limestone, quartzite, red, dark and green shale, dolerite, metallic ores and later coal measures. The volcanic rocks near Nuneaton contain important fossils laid down when England was located near the Antarctic Circle and they have been dated to 615 Ma. The Precambrian period represents over 4,500 million years of the Earth's history from the point of its formation to the appearance of the first animals with shells, roughly 600 Ma. These rocks are faulted against the adjoining Triassic mudstones and present a steep scarp slope to the Mease Lowlands to the north east along the River Mease. In the area to the north of Coventry, the ancient Precambrian rocks of the Hartshill ridge rose above the mudflats. Quartzite and flint pebbles occurring in the boulder clay were used by early man to make tools.

The next geological period of Silurian rocks is not represented in Warwickshire and Devonian rocks are confined to the narrow strip to the north-west of Nuneaton.

Arden – Carboniferous

The Carboniferous period (around 350 Ma to 300 Ma) is the time during which early tropical forests and swamps were forming and eventually became what are now known as the coal measures. The coal seams alternate with sandstones and clays, as the land was successively inundated with river deltas and tropical seas and sediment settled.

Between Kenilworth, Tamworth and Nuneaton an island of these Carboniferous Coal Measures is either exposed or is relatively shallowly buried. These older rocks, which contain alternate layers of sandstones and coal, have been pushed upwards through the Triassic Mercia Mudstone and these soft mudstones have eroded away. The coal seams are near the surface in the North of the area, but run progressively deeper to the South. The economically important rocks of the Carboniferous Period, which contain the coal of the Warwickshire Coalfield, are found north of Coventry. The only working pit is now at Daw Mill near Arley. Kenilworth is on deeper coal measures which it was planned to exploit but when serious plans were being drawn up in the 1980s it was deemed to be uneconomic. Carboniferous rocks are cut off on the west by a major boundary fault which forms a pronounced edge to the plateau along the Blythe and Tame valleys. Around Kenilworth & Warwick are the older carboniferous period rocks of which the light grey material is known as Ashow Foundation.

GEOLOGY

Arden - Triassic

North West of the River Avon, beneath the former Forest of Arden, is a band of older rocks, variously called Triassic Mercia Mudstone, Keuper Marl, Keuper Red Sandstone or Arden Sandstone. The hilly areas in this region, have been created because of the variations in the hardness of these sandstones. These rocks date from 250 Ma to 200 Ma and fossils have been found in them suggesting that at one time they were sand flats in a hot and arid climate and they were formed when Warwickshire was experiencing this climate during late Triassic times, about 230 Ma. Layers of fine, red, wind-blown dust settled in a patchwork of shallow salt-lakes and sun-baked mudflats surrounding the area now occupied by the Warwickshire coalfield. The layers of dust are now preserved as beds of a tough red clay which is found in many parts of Warwickshire. It is said that the landscape at this time may have resembled the present surface of Mars. Remnants of the ancient landscape still exist. In some places, the red rocks are exposed amongst the greenery of modern Warwickshire, providing us with glimpses of an alien world such as Corley rocks which protrude from the soil like rotting teeth.

Coleshill is on a base of Arden sandstone capped with glacial sands and gravels and the rock below is Keuper Marl. Further south Alcester also has Keuper Marl under the town and to the west but there is Blue Lias limestone to the south east. The nearest limestone quarry to Alcester was at Temple Grafton and the boundary between Keuper Marl and Blue Lias is at Red Hill. Primrose Hill in Oversley near Alcester is an outcrop of Arden sandstone and water is plentiful in the sandstone to the west of the River Arrow. The brown sandstone at Kenilworth was used to build Kenilworth Castle and similar material was also used for many buildings in Coventry. There is a prominent sandstone outcrop at Seckington in the far north of the county.

A type of clay called Fuller's earth was found at Stockingford and this was used for cleansing and finishing cloth and wool. Another use for clay was for brickmaking at Nuneaton and there was also quarrying at Dosthill brickworks, now a popular scuba diving centre. There were also a number of small brickworks around the county using the local clay. Etruria Marl, which was extracted near Tamworth, was used for making stoneware such as drain-pipes and the Baggeridge Company currently extracts the same material for making Staffordshire blue bricks at Kingsbury.

The South Staffordshire and East Warwickshire plateaux are separated by an area of Triassic rocks covered by glacial drift.

The soil in the parish of Morton Bagot is mainly Lower Keuper Marls with a band of Arden Sandstone on a fault line with Upper Keuper Marls above. The Keuper Marls are reddish clay prone to slight water-logging.

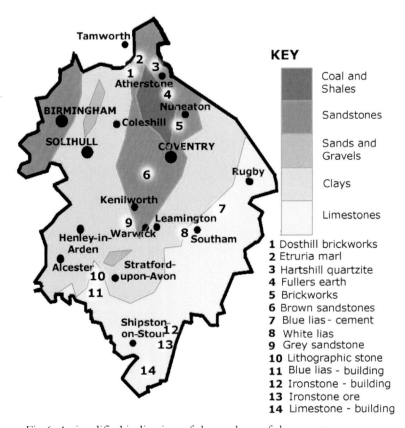

KEY

Coal and Shales

Sandstones

Sands and Gravels

Clays

Limestones

1 Dosthill brickworks
2 Etruria marl
3 Hartshill quartzite
4 Fullers earth
5 Brickworks
6 Brown sandstones
7 Blue lias - cement
8 White lias
9 Grey sandstone
10 Lithographic stone
11 Blue lias - building
12 Ironstone - building
13 Ironstone ore
14 Limestone - building

Fig 6. A simplified indication of the geology of the county

To the west of the county the geology of Birmingham is dominated by the Birmingham Fault which runs diagonally through the city from the Lickey Hills in the south west to Sutton Coldfield in the north east. To the south and east of the fault the ground is largely softer Keuper Marl, interspersed with beds of Bunter pebbles and crossed by the valleys of the Rivers Tame, Rea and Cole along with their tributaries. Much of this would have been laid down during the Permian and Triassic eras. To the north and west of the fault, varying from 45 to 180 metres (150 to 600 feet), higher than the surrounding area and underlying much of the city centre, lies a long ridge of harder Keuper Sandstone. Much of the area now occupied by the city was originally a northern reach of the ancient

Forest of Arden, the former presence of which can still be felt in the city's relatively dense oak tree-cover. It is also revealed in the large number of districts such as Moseley, Saltley and Hockley with names ending in '-ley': an Anglo-Saxon word meaning 'wood or woodland clearing'.

Summary of the Geography of Arden

To sum up, the coal deposits show that the entire area of Arden was, at one time, sub-tropical forest; the sandstone means that the entire area was once desert; the limestone deposits indicate that the area was, at some time, a warm shallow sea and the glacial deposits are evidence that the land was frequently covered with ice.

The result of this complex geology is that the area to the north and west of the River Avon is a moderately high rolling countryside known as Arden to the west and Dunsmore to the east with Mease uplands on the north eastern boundary. The Rivers Tame, Rea, Cole and Blythe in this area flow north into the River Trent which discharges in the Humber on the east coast. Some rivers in the south west, such as the Arrow and Alne, feed the River Avon which flows into the Severn which discharges on the west coast. The Arden plateau is capped with Keuper marls which are weathered to a broken topography with many streams. The small hills are due to outcrops of harder sandstone and glacial deposits

The younger rocks of the Jurassic period are a terracotta colour. In the outer region is the Mercia Mudstone. The dark brown material is Bromsgrove Sandstone, so-called because this same band of rocks occurs prominently near Bromsgrove. This porous stone forms the aquifer beneath Leamington which is the source of the spa waters.

In the North West is a band of glacial deposits, forming high ground in the area of Burton Green. This is called Oadby Till, named from a district in Leicestershire. The rock was carried here by glaciers coming down through Rugby and there is a large amount of glacial deposit in the Dunsmore area.

The soil in Arden is more acidic than in the south east and supports both sessile and pedunculate species of oak, lime and birch trees and holly, rowan and buckthorn in the undergrowth. Bracken is found on the sandy soils, for example in the Meriden area.

Feldon - South and East of the Avon Valley

The south, which has for a long time been known as Feldon, shows little evidence of rocks before the Permian period, about 300 million years ago, although the nearby areas of Kenilworth and Warwick do have slightly older Carboniferous rocks.

Feldon - Permian and Triassic

By 290 Ma Britain was at latitude 25 degrees North, typical of the present day Sahara or a Caribbean climate. Around 250 Ma (Triassic Period), the Mercia Sandstones were being formed from a sandy desert as described above for Arden. The Permian and Triassic periods are therefore represented by Keuper sandstones, which were used to build Kenilworth and Warwick castles, and red clays. These rocks underlie a large U-shaped area through the centre of the county forming the valleys of the Rivers Arrow and Avon.

Fig 7. Outcrops of rock in the county are rare but there are remains after quarrying at Burton Dassett Hills

Feldon - Jurassic

Much of southern Warwickshire is on top of layers of clay, limestone, sandstone and ironstone dating back to the Jurassic Period (200 Ma to 150 Ma). The rock beds are occasionally seen in quarries, road cuttings and other excavations. Harder rocks such as limestones and ironstones tend to cap the hills and ridges. Examples include the Burton Dassett Hills and Edge Hill. The abandoned quarry forms a large feature on Burton Dassett Hills Country Park (see Fig 7). Limestones can be seen at Cross Hands Quarry. The softer lias clays form the lowlands.

Clay and limestone beds, termed 'Blue Lias', were quarried at Harbury and Stockton and are still quarried for the manufacture of cement at Southam. In the past these beds yielded the skeletons of ichthyosaurs and plesiosaurs - real Jurassic sea-dragons. Hornton Stone to the south is slightly younger than the Blue Lias and it is a bed of rusty ironstone, quarried for building stone around Edge Hill and for ironstone at Radway, Ratley, Tysoe, Burton Dassett and Kineton.

The Vale of the Red Horse below Edge Hill, around Tysoe and Oxhill, is a string of gravel patches and glacial deposits which is the valley of the River Stour. This rock formed as iron-rich sand in a shallow current-swept coastal area. This formed the colour of the well-known horse cut into the hillside in the Vale of the Red Horse near Tysoe until around 1910.

The iron associated with the limestone indicates the former presence of rusty-coloured tropical soil on islands in the Jurassic period. These covered much of central England at that time. This type of limestone is called 'Oolitic'. This name does not refer to a marine creature, but is a physical precipitation of calcium carbonate, although it does frequently include marine fossils. The limestones of the Cotswolds are typical of this formation. The fossils found in the Jurassic rocks are the remains of creatures that lived in the ancient seas. The shells of ammonites and other sea-creatures including 'Devils' toenails' are the most common and bullet-like belemnites which are the internal shell of extinct squid-like animals are also found. The limestone areas are typically rolling uplands dissected by deep river valleys.

Oolitic limestone is also found at Long Compton and White Lias stone occurs around Loxley and Lighthorne and has been used for building. Blue Lias stone is present in Binton and Bidford-on-Avon and a very fine grained lithographic stone used for printing was extracted at Wilmcote.

To the south west of the county the Vale of Evesham is mainly Lower Lias clay with ribbings of Keuper marl and these porous deposits and relatively dry climate encourage fruit and vegetable growing.

In the far South East of the county is a still younger band, the Edge Hill escarpment. This is called Middle Lias and it is an approximately 50 metres (150 feet) thick band of brown sandstones, laid down around 150 Ma.

In the extreme South East is the edge of the Cotswold escarpment, which is an even younger band of Jurassic Limestone, dating from 140 Ma.

There are large areas of 'young' glacial deposits which are, by contrast to the bedrock, less than 1 million years old. After the Ice Ages the landscape was glacial debris, alluvium and lakes with tundra vegetation. Ice retreated in the late Devonian period (about 315 Ma). They are represented by extensive deposits of clay, sand and gravel. Some of these are important economically and a number of sand and gravel pits have been opened such as at Bubbenhall and Brandon.

Chesterton is mostly Keuper Marl with Lias clay further up the valley and some outcrops of limestone. Lapworth has generally poor land, only used for grazing and 'Hungry' Grafton (Temple Grafton) is so-named because of the very poor soil and, consequently, unproductive land.

Summary of the Geography of Feldon

The Lower Lias clays in south Warwickshire are generally heavy, poorly drained soils but they are more fertile than soils in the north. The clays give a flat or gently undulating scenery. There are distinct narrow parallel ridges of glacial origin between Wootton Wawen and Snitterfield. In the far south the undulating hills of the Cotswolds begin.

Overall the soil in Feldon is less acidic than Arden in the north-west and ash trees, the pedunculate oak, dogwood, hazel, the wayfaring tree and hawthorn tend to thrive.

About 500,000 years ago, the River Avon was a small river which drained northwards to the River Trent. Ice advanced from the north, east and west and the flow of the Avon to the north was blocked. The waters became impounded by the ice and the Cotswolds to the south, creating a large glacial lake, now called Lake Harrison. It is estimated that Lake Harrison covered the whole of Warwickshire and was over two hundred feet deep. After about 100,000 years the water was able to escape to the south-west, so forming the present day route of the River Avon. The Rivers Arrow, Alne, Sowe, Leam and Stour flow into the River Avon then on towards the River Severn which flows to the sea in the Bristol Channel on the west coast. The county as a whole therefore drains in two directions. Some rivers flow roughly to the north-east and the others to the south-west.

In the far south Ebrington Hill, on the fringe of the Cotswolds, is the highest point in the county at 259 metres (850 feet).

The table, or Timeline, which appears in Fig 8 below relates the geological periods to the number of years since they occurred in Britain and summarises which rock types are present in Arden and Feldon.

GEOLOGICAL TIMELINE

Millions of Years Ago (Ma)	Primary Geological Period	Secondary Geological Period	North & West	South and East
4500 to 615	Precambrian		Volcanic narrow ridge between Nuneaton & Atherstone, Huge quarries near Nuneaton, Quartzite quarried at Hartshill	Not present
615 to 500	Palaeozoic	Cambrian	Hartshill sandstone Stockingford shale	Not present
500 to 450	Palaeozoic	Ordovician	Stockingford shale	Not present
450 to 415	Palaeozoic	Silurian	Pebbles found in Carboniferous	Not present
415 to 350	Palaeozoic	Devonian	Not present	Not present

Millions of Years Ago (Ma)	Primary Geological Period		North & West	South and East
350 to 300	Palaeozoic	Carboniferous	Coal in a strip from Tamworth to Kenilworth. With layers of sandstone	Not present south of Warwick
300 to 250	Palaeozoic	Permian	Not present	Not present
250 to 220	Mesozoic	Triassic	Triassic Mercia Mudstone - also called Keuper Marl, Keuper Red Sandstone, and Arden Sandstones. Runs from Tamworth to Warwick. Also forms the Birmingham plateau	Sandstone
200 to 150	Mesozoic	Jurassic	Not present	Lower lias Oolite
140 to 150	Mesozoic	Late Jurassic	Not present	Limestone at Cotswold fringe – much of south / Middle Lias – Edge Hill escarpment

Millions of Years Ago (Ma)	Primary Geological Period	Secondary Geological Period	North & West	South and East
150 to 70	Mesozoic	Cretaceous	Not present	Not present
70 to 25	Tertiary	Palaeocene Eocene Oligocene Iocene Pliocene	Not present	Not present
25 to 2	Quaternary	Pleistocene	Glacial clays, sand & gravels	Glacial clays, sand & gravels
2 Ma	Quaternary	Holocene	Sands and gravels in river valleys eg river Tame	River terrace deposits eg River Avon

Fig 8. Geological Timeline

Chapter Two

The Stone Ages
500,000 BC to 2,400 BC

Introduction

About two million years ago mammals that we would probably recognise as men evolved in Africa and more recognisable human beings probably lived from about 700,000 years ago. It is likely that there were men in Britain from about 500,000 BC but the evidence is scanty because archaeological finds and features are rare and those that are found cannot be dated accurately. Many finds are simply said to be Prehistoric, that is created in the years before the Romans arrived in 43 AD. This Prehistoric period includes the Stone Ages, the Bronze Age and the Iron Age.

In the period referred to as the Stone Ages there were few humans in Europe. There were a number of cycles of Ice Ages when thick ice fields and glaciers covered the land and the people retreated from Britain and parts of Europe and only returned when it became warmer and there was a sufficient food supply available. Three Stone Ages are generally recognized. They are the Old Stone Age from 500,000 to 8,500 BC, the Middle Stone Age from 8,500 to 4,000 BC and the New Stone Age from 4,000 to 2,400 BC. These Stone Ages were followed by the Bronze Age and the Iron Age.

Old Stone Age or Palaeolithic Period – 500,000 BC to 8,500 BC

During the Old Stone Age small groups of humans probably roamed a thickly wooded landscape (the wildwood) in Britain in search of food. It is likely that they ate foods of plant origin and killed animals to eat. They used simple stone tools such as hand-axes and scrapers. Some estimates are that the total population of the county of Warwickshire may have been as low as 40 people. There is one piece of evidence of a temporary camp site at Waverley Wood Farm Quarry Pit at Bubbenhall where a stone implement made of andesite was discovered deep within the quarry. This has been dated as 500,000 years old. Elsewhere, particularly in north Warwickshire, large numbers of hand-axes have been found suggesting repeated visits to the sites. There have been finds indicating human activity from 10,000 BC at Hartshill. This Old Stone Age phase ended with the beginning of the Ice Ages, a very long period of time from which there is no evidence of humans in Warwickshire. All surface traces of man which may affect the appearance of the landscape have been erased by movement of ice and glaciers. The present landscape therefore reveals only evidence of the work of the glaciers and the effects of wind and water.

The Ice Ages

Parts of Britain were periodically covered by ice up to 2 kilometres thick over nearly half a million years and there is much evidence that stones of various types were brought to Warwickshire from elsewhere in Britain, such as the Lake District, by the movement of glaciers. In the vicinity of Long Compton it is estimated that the Ice ages left up to 15 feet depth of topsoil. It is generally accepted that the Ice Ages ended about 8,500 BC when the final phase of ice gradually melted away. It is likely that shrubs, trees and other plants became established from 11,000 BC. The lime tree was probably the first species to take root in England.

Middle Stone Age or Mesolithic Period - 8,500 to 4,000 BC

As the ice disappeared and vegetation became established again humans and other animals returned to Warwickshire from about 8,500 BC at the beginning of the Middle Stone Age or Mesolithic period. However opinions do differ and some authorities believe settlement was as late as 4,000 BC. As the climate became warmer and the ice sheets retreated, habitats changed as the forest was re-established. It is believed that the climate of England was fairly stable from 6,500 to 400 BC which encouraged settlement.

These early humans were hunter-gatherers who used bows and arrows and had domesticated dogs to help them in the chase for meat for the table. Vegetable foods such as nuts, roots and berries would also have formed an important part of their diet. Flint tools were used for cleaning skins and working wood and bone. This period is noted for the use of microliths which were small delicately worked stone points set into arrow-shafts. Some twenty Middle Stone Age sites are known in Warwickshire of which the most important is Blacklow Hill, near Warwick. Excavations here have revealed a substantial tool-making site. Other sites which are known in the Avon valley and also in the Nuneaton area have produced a large number of finds and evidence of several settlement sites from this period. Warwickshire County Council archeologists have records of about 500 finds and surface marks to show Middle and New Stone age inhabitants between 8,500 BC and 43 AD. These sites are inconspicuous but can be identified by diligent research.

Fig 9. An "ancient" footpath at Lillington

New Stone Age or Neolithic Period - 4,000 to 2,400 BC

Around 4,000 BC the hunter-gatherer way of living gradually evolved into a simple farming economy, thus further modifying the landscape as the wildwood was removed piece by piece. It is possible that the clearance of the woodland began in a piecemeal fashion from 3,000 to 4,000 BC. Wheat and barley were cultivated in the Fertile Crescent in the area of Mesopotamia from as early as 16,000 BC and the skills were probably carried to Britain around 4,000 BC. It is believed that the soil was being tilled in the Coleshill area from 4,000 BC. The name of the original clearings in the woods was 'feld', meaning that trees had been 'felled' and eventually led to the present use of the word 'field'. These New Stone Age or Neolithic people raised sheep, pigs and cattle, and grew cereal crops. The earliest crops were wheat and barley but later rye, oats, spelt and flax were grown along with fruits such as apples, cherries & plums. 'Spelt' was a variety of wheat grown from these times until the Medieval period and it is still available now. The people used stone tools, axes and fire to make clearings in the woodland where they could build farms and lay out fields. Burning was used to kill off old woody material that sheep and other animals could not eat. The great effort required for the removal of tree roots should be recognised. A particular feature of woodland management which developed at this period was 'coppicing'. This process involves removing

26

branches for use from a tree at a young age and this is followed by regeneration of the branches over 10 to 20 years which are then cut again. The result is a large base or stool from which many branches grow and this process is repeated a number of times. The resulting branches or long twigs were used for a number of purposes, including the construction of shelters. Coppicing continues to this day for the production of wood for the manufacture of charcoal and for making interwoven panels. Evidence of ancient woodbanks or boundaries survives at Hartshill Hayes, Clowes Wood (Earlswood), Ryton Wood, Hampton Wood and Windmill Naps Wood (south of Birmingham). Around 3,500 BC people started to enclose the land with fences and ditches and to live in semi-permanent sites. From 1,500 BC land boundaries were established for groups of people living together. There is evidence of the shape of some of these early clearings in the Arden area.

Fig 10. A view at Offchurch

Evidence of the use of a variety of stone implements is found in flint mines and stone axe quarries which date from 3,200 to 2,200 BC. There was probably some quarrying and trading in stone from as early as 4,500 BC and there were lithic works (places where stone implements were made) at Chesterton and Hillmorton. In addition there are over 100 sites of flint scatters known in the county. Odd flints and neolithic stone artefacts have been found near to Alcester and a chisel shaped axe head or 'celt' has been found at Long Compton. Stone age implements have also been found in the Nuneaton area.

In Warwickshire there were a large number of Stone Age settlements along the valley of the River Avon and they extended from the source right down to Tewkesbury. These people evidently found it easy to cultivate the light sand and gravel of the terraces of the Avon for food production.

Much of the remaining evidence of the presence of humans on the land in Warwickshire at this time is in the form of commemoration of death. In Britain in general monumental communal tombs were constructed from 4,000 to 3,200 BC and the later Neolithic henges were built from 3,200 to 2,200 BC. The ritual burial evidence in Warwickshire is mostly in the west. There were individual burials from 3,200 to 1,600 BC and stone circles were built to mark the tombs. Henges are generally roughly circular areas enclosed by a ditch and exterior bank about 20 metres in diameter. They are believed to have a ritual purpose but details are unknown. These tombs and henges have left vestigial marks on the landscape best seen in aerial photographs when the sun is low in the sky. Stone Age burial sites have been investigated at Stretton-under-Fosse, Kings Newnham and Barford and possible sites of henges are at Barford, Kings Newnham, Wasperton, Copston Magna and Wolvey.

Fig 11. The Rollright Stones. The overcast sky accentuates the mystery of the site

Other features which may date from this time are barrows or mounds and six Neolithic long barrows are suggested at Charlecote, Alderminster, Brailes,

Ilmington, Little Compton and Lighthorne. There are also 10 burnt mounds, which are evidence of cremation, across the county from Middleton and Wishaw in the north to Baddesley Clinton and Chesterton in the south. The impressive stone circle at Rollright Stones, which is said to be around 3,000 BC, is on the southern border of Warwickshire in the northern Cotswolds and it is believed to have had a ritual purpose.

It is likely that the construction of primitive causeways, bridges and fords began at some time during this period by the simple use of timber and stone, although there is no evidence to show that any such structures ever existed in the county.

These were dangerous times for men. Wild beasts which would have been encountered in the landscape in prehistory in Britain included lions, elephant, leopard, hyena, rhinoceros, hippopotamus, cave bear, Irish elk, sabre-toothed cat, bear, beaver, wolf, wild swine, crane, polecat, marten, wildcat, European bison (or wisent) and auroch (plural aurochsen).

Chapter Three

The Bronze Age
2,400 BC to 600 BC

The Evidence

The long period of the Stone Ages merged gradually into the Bronze Age around 2,400 BC and this era lasted until the Iron Age began around 600 BC. The period is habitually divided into the Early Bronze Age which ran from 2,400 to 1,500 BC and the Later Bronze Age from 1,500 to 600 BC. The naming of the Bronze Age relates to the fact that people were able to make bronze and use it to manufacture things; this happened before people were able to extract iron.

The traditional assumption was that Warwickshire was virtually all covered with oak woodland with scarcely any clearance at this time but now it is believed that a significant area of the county had been cleared for agriculture especially in the Feldon area to the south and east. It is likely that as time passed other areas of woodland were cleared and farmed. When crop yields fell on a particular plot it is likely that nearby areas were cleared and, to some extent, there was re-growth of woodland on the newly abandoned land. The result of this was that at the end of the Bronze Age the landscape as we know it today was probably fairly well developed and may have been recognisable to us today.

Early Bronze Age - 2,400 to 1,500 BC
Extent of Woodlands, Field Patterns

During this period the clearance of woodland probably intensified and enabled the lifestyle of the people to become more pastoral. There is little evidence of significant building from this time apart from burial barrows and light timber dwellings but in other parts of the country, such as Somerset and Lancashire, timber track-ways through marshland have been found. There are around 30 round barrows from the Bronze age in the county and there is evidence of Celtic style fields at Coleshill around 2,000BC. The Rollright stone circle near Long Compton may also have been a Bronze Age construction. In the

Long Compton area there were early Bronze age camps at Tadmarton, Rainsborough, Arberry Hill and Castle Hill at Brailes. This demonstrates that there was considerable organisation within the communities and a strong determination to improve the environment for living at this time.

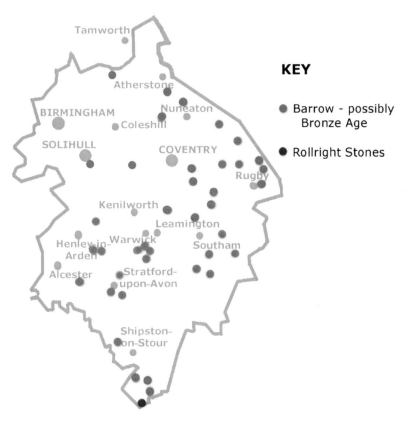

Fig12. Bronze Age sites

Later Bronze Age - 1,500 to 600 BC
Barrows and Hillforts

The period from 1,500 BC onwards is often known as the time of the Celtic fields which lasted into the Roman times after AD 43. This was a continuing period of mixed farming including primarily wheat and barley, cattle and sheep.

People lived in simple farmsteads rather than in clustered villages and the dwellings were circular in form. The only traces found of these dwellings today are usually post holes. Land boundaries such as ditches and fences also became much more common during this time.

Barrow sites were used for human burials in the Bronze Age and at least 50 have been found in the county including examples at Ansley, Hartshill, Gaydon, Chesterton, Bishops Itchington, Napton, Old Stratford and Stratford-upon-Avon.

Fig 13. View across the River Avon near Sherbourne.
The same scene in flood is in Fig 94

Oldbury Camp near Hartshill can still be traced and there are barrow sites on high land in Morton Bagot. These barrow burials used to be referred to as a component of the Wessex Culture in the early days of nineteenth century archaeology and were typified by the barrows in southern England which contained valuable grave goods. The term Wessex Culture is now little used.

Although hill forts are known in other parts of England from the Bronze Age those in Warwickshire are generally considered as being from the Iron Age era.

Chapter Four

The Iron Age
600 BC to 43 AD

Lack of Evidence, The Wildwood

The Bronze Age merged into the Iron Age around 600 BC and there was a further period of gradual change in the utilization of the land although the evidence of what the countryside looked like in detail at that time is now largely well hidden. Virtually the only evidence is the earthworks which exist from this period which are the remains of hill forts. The people who inhabited the county at this time are usually referred to as Celts.

Much of the woodland in Feldon and some of that in Arden had been cleared for farming in the Iron Age and some of the resulting timber was used for fuel in the Midlands ironworks. Knowledge about this period is limited and published information is confusing. Most sources give estimates that the area of farmland was around 3% of today's farmland but one other source suggests that there was less woodland in the Iron Age than there is today. It seems unlikely that the small population at this time would have the resources to clear more land than needed. It has also been estimated that in about 300 BC around 20 acres of woodland were required to feed one farmstead. The farmland was usually enclosed by low banks which was typical for the regular enclosed Celtic fields. Signs of some of these Celtic fields were found before the construction of the Kenilworth bypass (A46). Farming in the Iron Age included autumn-sown cereals and nuts and, in addition, berries and fungi were harvested. Sheep and Cattle used winter pasture and provided manure which was used on harvested fields. The use of coppiced woodland also continued.

Industry, Settlement

'Industry' in a primitive form had begun. During this period tiles were produced at Kenilworth, Lapworth and Nuneaton and pottery was made at Alcester, Mancetter and in the Hartshill area. This latter embryonic 'industry' was spread over about 4 square miles. It is likely that some of the pottery and tiles which were produced were transported for some distance across the country either along the rivers or by packhorse. Another significant example of long distance transport at this time was that of salt from Droitwich which moved along a road into the county at Alcester which was used for many centuries and is still known today as the Saltway. Salt was very important for preserving food. There was trading over quite long distances and a number of roads were created. The ancient Jurassic Way was a route which ran along the top of Edge Hill and this was part of a long distance route from the Humber to Salisbury Plain. The present footpath known as the Jurassic Way follows a parallel route and goes from Banbury to Stamford just beyond the Warwickshire boundary.

Fig 14. The view to the north from Edge Hill over the rooftops of houses in Arlescote from a location near the Iron Age Camp at Nadbury

Medieval estates in Feldon to the south of the county were linked to more areas in the wooded regions of the North, perhaps from the Iron Age. It is believed that in the autumn pigs were driven from Feldon to the woods in Arden to eat acorns and beech mast and there is remaining evidence of the tracks which were used.

There was a fairly dense pattern of settlement in the county well before the Romans came and the houses which were constructed were round and well-built from wood. There was probably an Iron Age settlement on the modern site of the University of Warwick. At least 18 Iron Age hill forts have been recorded in Warwickshire, including ten in the Avon Valley.

These earthworks and hut circles range from Coleshill, Polesworth and Corley in the north to Beausale and Alderminster in the south. There were also much larger sites at Oldbury camp, near Hartshill, and at Wappenbury. The earthworks at Wappenbury extend to 25 acres and were strongly defended to

34

protect the crossing of the River Leam and the site also shows evidence of settlement in the preceding Stone and Bronze ages. Aerial photographs also reveal Iron Age settlements around Alcester. There was a large hill fort at Nadbury camp, near Ratley, where the flat area stretches for 17 acres with twin ramparts surrounding it. This site dates from 500 BC and is on Edge Hill.

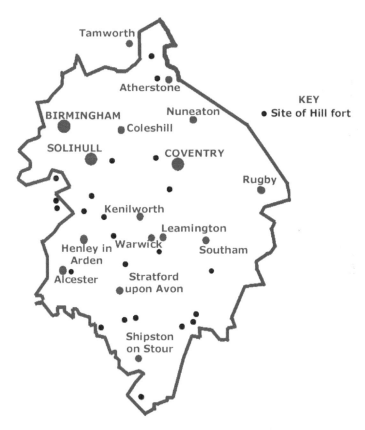

Fig 15. Iron Age hill forts

There is a triple ditch system in Priory Park at Warwick and an eroded bank and ditch to the north of Offchurch churchyard which are both from the Iron Age. There are linear earthworks at Blunts Green near Tanworth-in-Arden and the Berry Mound was an 11 acre Iron Age site at Solihull. There was a Celtic temple at Grimstock Hill near Coleshill which was later an extensive Roman site. Harborough banks, to the east of the canal at Kingswood, are the remains of a British and Roman camp. At Chesterton there is evidence from this time of a ridgeway road on the northern boundary, now called Beggars Lane.

Fig 16. Iron Age complex at Fenny Compton (Courtesy of Warwickshire Museum)

Fig 17. Possible Iron Age cropmarks at Ettington (Courtesy of Warwickshire Museum)

From 100 to 10 BC the area known as Hwicce included the southern half of Warwickshire and the north was in the area of the Coritani people. From 10 BC to 43 AD the Coritani or Corieltauvi moved to the north-east and Warwickshire was almost wholly in a tribal area called Dobunni. There is no striking evidence that the arrival of these new tribes had any impact on the way the land was used or its appearance.

Chapter Five

The Romans
43 AD to 410 AD

The Invasion, Woodland, Roman Evidence

It is well known that a key event in the history of England and Wales was the invasion by the Romans in the first century AD. They have left many marks on the landscape of Warwickshire which still remain. They arrived on the coast in 43 AD under the leadership of Aulus Plautius when Claudius was the emperor. However subjugation of the whole country took some time and the Warwickshire area was not under the total control of the Romans until around 60 AD and even in 61 AD there was a battle near Mancetter at about the same time that Boudicca was leading the Iceni in revolt against the Romans in the east. Some sources declare that Boudicca was killed in Warwickshire. Therefore it can be seen that for several years the Midlands, including Warwickshire, was a 'frontier zone'.

Again it is necessary to consider how much woodland was left in Warwickshire in Roman times although this is a matter of some debate. Life for the native population probably continued very much as it was for a while but as well as feeding themselves they were required to provide food and other supplies for the invaders. It is therefore likely that more land had to be brought into production by felling some of the woodlands. The Romans gradually revolutionised agriculture by levelling the Celtic banks and ditches around settlements and they also felled large areas of the remaining woodland for use to build fortifications in many locations. Roman fields were generally larger than Celtic ones. We have no evidence for the actual position of Roman field boundaries in the county. Around Coleshill there were fewer trees than later in medieval times and it is likely that the land around Gilson, Chelmsley Wood & Water Orton was well farmed at this time. Also the land in the Alcester area was probably well cultivated to produce a range of mixed grains and cattle, sheep and pigs were reared.

The main marks left behind by the Romans in the landscape of today are the towns, settlements, forts, quarries and roads. The native population was no doubt forced to help in building these constructions for the occupiers. The most obvious features left in the landscape today are the routes of the roads, although much other archaeological evidence of their presence has been found. The position of the roads has often subtly changed as routes had to be redrawn because of lack of maintenance. In some places the existing roads are now far from being as straight as the original route.

Roman Britain was initially divided into two parts. Britannia Superior was focused on the south with the capital in London and Britannia Inferior was in the north with the capital at York. Britannia Superior included the areas of the Cornovii and Dobunni tribes who occupied parts of southern Warwickshire whereas the Corieltauvi, who from time to time occupied north Warwickshire, were in Britannia Inferior governed from York. Therefore the government of Warwickshire by the Romans was split between London and York. The capital for the Dobunni tribal area was in Corinium, the present-day Cirencester. By the fourth century Roman Britain was further divided and the west was named Britannia Prima, again with the capital at Cirencester.

Much of Arden was neglected by the Romans. They preferred to settle on sandy soils which were easier to work. It is unclear to what extent the clay soils were cultivated at this time. Unfortunately all evidence of Roman agriculture has been lost under later ploughing.

Fig 18. The Fosse Way (Photo on the left courtesy of Warwickshire Museum)

Roman Roads, Settlements

Roman roads are much in evidence in Warwickshire. They were used for troop movements and movement of supplies but also, as life evolved above subsistence level, there was trade in many goods such as tiles and pottery. The two primary routes in the county were Watling Street and the Fosse Way. Watling Street in Roman times ran from London to Wroxeter near Shrewsbury. It forms much of the north-eastern boundary of Warwickshire and the settlements of High Cross, Tripontium and Mancetter were established along the route in Warwickshire. The Fosse Way ran from Exeter to Lincoln and the settlements of Chesterton and Brinklow were on the route.

A less important road was Ryknild (or Icknield) Street which ran from Bourton-on-the-Water in Gloucestershire to Templeborough in Yorkshire passing through Alcester (it should not be confused with the Icknield *Way* which runs from Buckinghamshire to Norfolk). A preserved section of Ryknild Street can be seen at Sutton Park at Sutton Coldfield. At Alcester there is a crossroads where Ryknild Street crosses the Saltway from Droitwich towards Stratford-on-Avon. There was also a minor Roman road from Leicester by way of Mancetter, Hartshill, Exhall, Coventry, Baginton and Wappenbury to Chesterton. There is also evidence of a Roman causeway at Coventry.

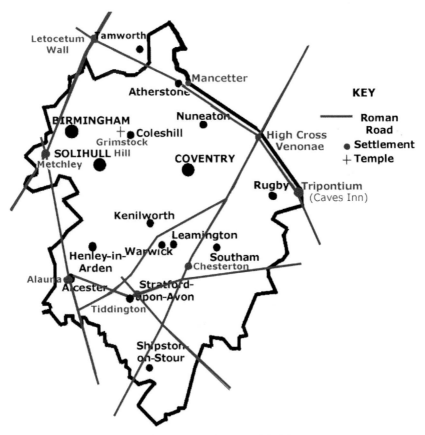

Fig 19. The Romans in Warwickshire

The Romans marked every thousand double steps with a marker which was a cylindrical stone. About 120 of these still exist, mostly in museums. None are known in Warwickshire but there are two in Leicestershire.

As a very general rule it is said that most of the people lived in smaller settlements approximately 2 kilometres apart. Roman villas dominated the West Midlands and considerable evidence has been found of about 15 of them in the Avon valley. In the vicinity of Kineton there was a Roman villa at Brookhampton and another Romano-British settlement just outside the present town on the Banbury Road. Some of today's parishes probably still retain the boundaries of the Roman estates. There were a number of Roman settlements in the area of Alcester and the Arrow valley. There were at least 20 villas in Alcester and Roman mosaics, roof tiles and painted plaster have been found along the valley of the River Arrow. From around 1600 it has been recorded that Alcester was initially named Alauna by the Romans but later the town became known as Alcestria. Alcester became one of 80 to 100 small Roman towns in Britain and it was about 30 hectares (72 acres) in extent. There was a Roman fort at Lower Oversley Lodge near Alcester. The Roman garrison probably left Alcester before 75 AD to move further north. The parts of the Roman street plan of Alcester which have been excavated do not follow the present pattern of streets. There is now an excellent Roman museum in Alcester run by the county council. Tiddington near Stratford-upon-Avon, is believed to have been a small subsidiary settlement to Alcester.

Fig 20. Roman walls excavated at Alcester   Fig 21. Roman mosaic floor at Chesterton

(Both photos courtesy of Warwickshire Museum)

In Celtic times Grimstock (Grimscot) Hill at Gilson, near Coleshill, initially consisted of about five circular huts and the site continued to be used as a Roman settlement. In Roman times the settlement on the hill was built as a square within a square and it also had a Roman temple and a bath house. The temple was a wooden building in the second century but was made of stone by the fourth century. The layout of the settlement was altered in the third century and it became one of the largest in Britain. It may have been important because it was on the boundary between the Cornovii centred on Wroxeter and the

Coritani based in Leicester. Many finds have confirmed the existence of this settlement and these include wells, a Roman wall and many Roman artefacts including coins, a brooch, a pendant, a bracelet, pottery, bricks and tiles.

Fig 22. Excavations and artist's impression of a Roman temple at Grimstock Hill.
(Pictures courtesy of Warwickshire Museum)

There is a great deal of evidence of Roman settlement in Coventry. A Roman pavement and coins have been found under Broadgate and a hoard of 18,000 Roman copper coins was found in 1792 in Foleshill. Another find in Coventry was a Roman statue of Mars. It is likely that the name of Coventry derives from Coventina, who was a Roman water goddess. There is also the Roman Lunt Fort at nearby Baginton which has been partly reconstructed.

Chesterton was a small Roman camp and had around 20 villas together with extensive fortifications including a 100 feet ditch in the fourth century. Evidence has been found of two villas at Ewefields Farm and Lodge Clump. A Roman villa has also been found at Radford Semele. There was extensive Roman occupation at Atherstone and nearby Mancetter near to Watling Street. There was also a Roman farm at Kings Norton in the far west of the county.

Relics of Roman forts have been found at Baginton, Budbrooke, Clifford Chambers and Metchley (on the campus of the University of Birmingham at Edgbaston). Other Roman sites are a fort at Camp Hill in Nuneaton and a fort called Wall at Sutton Park. There is also the major site at Tripontium or Roman Caves Inn at Shawell near Churchover on Watling Street and a Romano-British enclosure at Broadwell. Near to Nuneaton the Roman settlement of Manduessadum was near Mancetter.

There was a Roman settlement at High Cross was at the crossroads of Watling Street and Fosse Way, known by the Romans as Venonae. There were also villas at Butlers Marston, Gaydon, Kineton, Leek Wootton, Lighthorne,

Long Compton, Long Itchington, Luddington, Pillerton Priors, Sambourne, Warwick and Welford on Avon.

Many of these settlements and forts have left features in the landscape which have been excavated but now most of them need aerial photography or a good archaeological imagination to recognise them.

Industry, The Romans Leave

The Romans were more developed in various skills of manufacturing than the Celts. It is possible that Griff near Bedworth was the site of a Roman coalmine because 'graefan' in Anglo Saxon means 'to dig' and this may be the origin of the place name. There were also two Roman tile kilns at Griff and other tile kilns at Lapworth, Alcester and Kenilworth and there were also Roman pottery kilns at Mancetter, Wappenbury and Alcester. Evidence of pottery works at Tiddington and Wappenbury has also been found. These pottery and tile works were close to the road network which had been developed by the Romans and the products were distributed widely. The shops in the Roman towns, such as Alcester, sold a wide variety of goods including wine, oil, salt, tools, jewellery, glassware and pottery. The word tavern, one of the names for a public house, came from the Latin word *taverna* for an alehouse. There were water mills in Roman times at Guys Cliffe on the River Avon, Hoo Mill at Haselor on the River Alne and at Blackdown Mill also on the Avon.

The occupation of Britain by the Romans came to an end in 410 AD when they were being isolated by barbarian action on the continent and decided to cut their losses and return to the south. Even before this date the Romans did not have a peaceful time because there had already been Saxon raids from the south and south east from around 200 AD and the Picts and Scottis were active in opposition in the north and west from 367 AD.

Chapter Six

Saxons and Vikings
410 to 1066

Introduction

This chapter covers a lengthy period of over 650 years stretching from the departure of the Romans to the arrival of the Normans. Documentary and physical evidence of what the countryside looked like and how changes have affected the current landscape is again very scarce. There is clear evidence that there were significant movements of people during this period and it is likely that there were some advances in agriculture and other aspects of land use. Unfortunately very little now remains of these endeavours because of the labours of the many generations which have followed. Study of what we know about the general history of the time does give some indication of what was happening to the landscape at this time.

We will therefore examine the impact of the Anglo Saxons and the Vikings on the history of the county. It is often difficult at this distance in time to disentangle the impact of the Angles and Saxons from the later arrivals, the Vikings, although the latter are, perhaps unfairly, generally perceived as more warlike than pastoral.

Anglo-Saxon Occupation, Settlements

As the Romans departed from Britain the land was initially left to be governed by the native British or Celts. The post Roman period has been referred to by a number of different names. The period from 410 until 1066 is often called the Early Medieval period and the Late Medieval period is from 1066 to 1500. Because the total length of this medieval period has left remarkably few obvious traces on the ground or in writings it is also known as the Dark Ages. At this time there was a great movement of people around mainland Europe and into and out of Britain and therefore this time is also referred to by many historians as the Migration Period.

The situation is quite complex and confusing. The Angles and Saxons began to arrive in significant numbers around 450 after several earlier attacks on the Romans before 410, although some of the earlier Anglo Saxons had actually

43

been employed as Roman mercenaries. Anglo Saxons came from north western Europe and first settled in the south east of Britain after arriving in open boats. They migrated further afield into England from around 500. They established their own settlements as they pushed west, reaching the Fosse Way by about 600. The Anglo Saxon Chronicles which were begun in 890 by King Alfred of Mercia (later King Alfred the Great) refer to only one settlement in north Warwickshire before 750 and another two in the following one hundred years. Even more disappointing is that the writings of Bede (who died in 735) have nothing at all to say about Warwickshire but they do mention Lichfield to the north and Malmesbury to the south so it is safe to assume that the land in between these towns was quite densely populated.

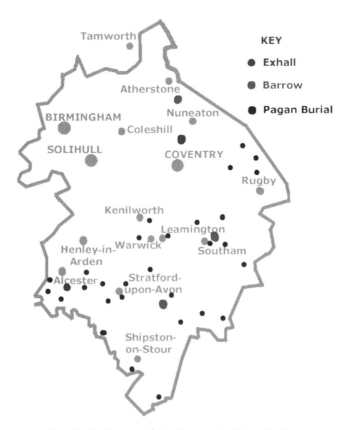

Fig 23. Evidence of the Saxons in Warwickshire

The Anglo Saxons arrived in Warwickshire in two main groups, one from the south and another from the north-east. Those from the north were called the

South Mercians and those from the south were from the Hwicce tribe. There was a tussle for power and the South Mercians overwhelmed the Hwicce tribe in about 650. However the struggle between the north and the south of the county continued for many more years and the boundary between the major tribes shifted frequently in the seventh century. The final boundary has been largely preserved in that which still exists between the present ecclesiastical dioceses of Lichfield and Worcester.

It is likely that the Anglo-Saxons chose to settle in areas where there were already existing communities of Romano-Britons. Although the Anglo Saxons were invaders it is likely that the two groups soon exchanged ideas and customs and they eventually combined to form a new people. There is little physical evidence of the sites of settlements in Warwickshire from this time but burial sites have been found in the Avon valley at Bidford-on-Avon, Wasperton and Warwick and also in the Stour valley at Stretton-on-Fosse. These burials contained weapons and jewellery and were probably made in the hundred years before Christianity was widespread. It is necessary to be wary because some mounds which at first suggest burial places actually appear to have been used as the focal point of meeting places.

A cheerful sign to be seen in the landscape at this time was a green bush up a pole which indicated a Saxon alehouse. However in 965 King Edgar decreed that there should be only one alehouse in each village.

One local claim to fame is that King Ethelbald was murdered in 757 at Seckington in the north of the county.

The Vikings
Invasion, Social Structure, Feudalism

The first recorded raid by the Vikings on Britain was at Lindisfarne Island in 793 and this was followed much later by an invasion in 866 when the Great Army of Vikings landed to make a serious effort to occupy Britain. As soon as they had a foothold the Vikings began to break up the estates which had developed especially to the east of Warwickshire. In Coventry there are two Danish place names, Biggin in Stoke and Keresley, which indicate the presence of the Vikings at some time. In the eighth century the main settlement in Coventry was either on Barrs Hill or in the valley between it and Broadgate Hill.

The Vikings forced their way into Warwickshire and the territory of Mercia in the north of the county lost much land to the Vikings around 874. In the Peace of Wedmore (also called the Treaty of Chippenham) in about 878 Alfred the Great negotiated that the Vikings could settle land to the north and east of Watling Street. This Viking area was known as Danelaw. The result of this treaty was that on the north and eastern boundaries of Warwickshire the Saxons met the Vikings at a border. Castles were built for defence against the Vikings at Tamworth and Warwick in 913 and 914 respectively. At this time the whole of the county was in Mercia which was closely linked to Wessex. Mercia did eventually become part of Wessex but it had a separate King Edgar from 957 to 959. In 1016 the Viking King Cnut harried and burnt his way through Warwickshire and as part of this his army destroyed the nunnery at Coventry. Mercia again had a separate existence in Cnut's time from 1020 and Warwickshire continued as part of Mercia. From about 1051 some lands were reallocated to the Vikings and Mercia became part of the Earldom of Leofric.

Throughout most of this lengthy period of time the areas used for administration were the 'hundreds' and most of these had a mound where leaders stood at meetings. There is the remains of a hundred mound near Sutton Coldfield and another at Dunsmore.

The county of Winchcombeshire was established by the Vikings from 1007 to 1017 and was situated to the south of the Avon and west of the Stour. It consisted of 139 parishes that were divided into 12 Hundreds. It stretched almost to the gates of Stratford-upon-Avon.

The main form of social organization in this period was what we now refer to as 'feudalism' although this term itself was not actually used until 1839. The feudal system was based primarily on land ownership and involved a hierarchy of authority, rights, and power that extended from the monarch downwards and the monarch owned all of the land in the country. Beneath the crown, an intricate network of duties and obligations linked royalty, tenants-in-chief (such as the barons), under-tenants (the knights), and villeins, serfs or peasants at the bottom. Feudalism was reinforced by personal oaths of allegiance and a complex legal system and it was also supported by the medieval Christian church.

In a further complication the monarch allowed powerful vassals (feudal tenants) to hold land in return for performing military service and often also conferred on them the right to administer justice and levy taxes. Vassals were first heard of in the ninth century. These vassals in turn could 'sublet' such rights, usually keeping part of the land (known as the demesne) for themselves.

At the bottom of the system were the villeins, who worked for free for a specified number of days each year on their lord's manor lands in return for being allowed to cultivate some land for themselves. The villeins' lives were undoubtedly hard but at least they could not be sold as if they were slaves. However they could not leave the estate to live or work elsewhere without permission. Their work was supervised on behalf of the lord of the manor by a village official called the reeve.

Later in the eighth century the land was mainly split between noblemen with a Caput as the most important house at the centre of an estate. Various names were used for the different categories of people throughout the Saxon period. In late Saxon and Viking times there were the King, Earls, Thegns or Thanes, Ceorls and Slaves. Later the common names in use were the King, Lords and Barons, Freemen, Villeins and Cottars. The feudal system lasted into Norman times until the 13th century, gradually giving way to the class system as the dominant form of social ranking. The title Villein was gradually replaced by Yeoman after feudalism ended. There were also officials called Ealdormen or magistrates in Warwickshire by 970.

Territories

As we have seen the two main groups of people in the county were the Mercians and Hwicce. The territory of a small tribe called Stoppingas was in central Warwickshire and it was based on Wootton Wawen and was within the Hwicce area. This village has an Anglo Saxon church which is described later. In 650 north Warwickshire was the home of the Tomsaetan (the Tame dwellers) based in the Tame & Blythe Valleys whereas to the south west were the Arosaetna who held 600 hides (a hide is about 120 acres) in the Arrow valley.

After the Romans left Britain the territory of Hwicce had the same boundaries as the Worcester diocese and roughly covered the Severn Valley and Northern Cotswolds. South Warwickshire was therefore within Hwicce area before the end of the eighth century and the capital of Hwicce was at Worcester. The name of the Hwicce tribe may be remembered in the village name of Whichford in the south of the county but this is uncertain because the derivation may alternatively come from 'wych', another name for the elm tree.

From the sixth century there were Anglo Saxons in the Nuneaton area in the valleys of the Rivers Anker and Sowe. This settlement was known as Ea-Tun which later evolved to the present name. This all demonstrates that there was widespread settlement in the county at this time. It may well be that these separate tribes had different ways of using the land but information has been lost.

The Middle Angles came from the east in about 625 and the River Avon became the boundary between Mercia to the west and the Middle Angles to the east. Hwicce became incorporated into Mercia from about 650 to 700. For example, Kineton, Chadshunt, Burton Dassett and Radway were at one time in Hwicce and later were in south Mercia. Mercia dominated from 725 to 825 and then Wessex further to the south began to take over Mercia.

Events are clearer from the seventh century because there were written charters which defined areas of land and who owned them.

During the tenth century the West Saxons extended the division of the land into shires to Mercia and these were based on Burhs such as Warwick and thus Warwickshire was created and christened. By 1066 most of England was already divided into parishes.

Warwickshire used the land measures of hides and hundreds whereas the Vikings in Danelaw to the north and east used the names of wapentakes and carucates. The administrative areas of Warwickshire were the hundreds and the ancient Demesnes which remained separate. See page 63 for more details of the hundreds.

Settlements, Languages

Despite the lack of significant physical evidence from this time there are present-day aerial photographs and the charters and boundary descriptions from this period which show that the countryside was full of people, settlements and farms with only a few truly remote uninhabited areas in Warwickshire.

Medieval settlements are referred to by various names during this period including parishes, manors, tithings and burhs. These small Anglo Saxon townships formed the basis of later ecclesiastical parishes and many of them had the same boundaries as the administrative parishes which we still know today. We will see that in later periods some of the modern parish boundaries have been adjusted to include deserted or shrunken parishes. From the ninth century there was a growing concentration of people at centres (hamlets, villages or towns) in highly cultivated areas and this trend is known as 'nucleation'. This had a distinct impact on the appearance of the landscape. From 700 onwards it was customary for the name of an estate to be the earliest place name which was remembered for the location. Despite successive waves of conquest by Saxons, Vikings and Normans the area we know as Arden kept its British/Celtic name derived from the word 'ardu' which means steep or high. Some Saxon leaders had accumulated large estates but the Vikings took power and broke up many of these from the ninth century onwards.

It is impossible to list every settlement in Warwickshire so we will give a very brief story of a selection of places during this period. Where appropriate a likely derivation of a place name is also indicated although some of the derivations can be somewhat speculative.

'Ecles' is a Saxon name with an ecclesiastical derivation. This indicates that the two Exhalls near Coventry and Alcester almost certainly had religious connections in this period. It is important to note that towns expanded at different rates depending on local circumstances. For example Warwick expanded around the year 914, Southam was large enough to be granted a charter in 998 whereas the expansion of Coventry began much later in 1043.

Within the historic county of Warwickshire the most important Mercian royal vill (or town) in the eighth century was at Tamworth (later allocated to Staffordshire) under the rule of King Offa.

In the Anglo-Saxon period the village of Coleshill was in the Mercian province of Tomasaetan which had its capital at Tamworth. For some reason the nucleus of Coleshill moved from the bottom of the valley and up the hill during the Dark Ages. Coventry began as a Saxon village when it was called Coffantree, which means the tree belonging to Coffa (there is an alternative theory for a derivation from a Roman name). In Coventry the Babba Lacu was a large lake which stretched at this time from the present Hales Street to Hill Street before it was drained. Warwick was established in the seventh century and was fortified in 914 to prepare for the possibility of attack by Vikings. Warwick was the main town in the county in Saxon times and it covered about 57 acres in 920. It was one of the largest of the walled burhs in Britain at this date.

Stratford-upon-Avon started on a large area of river gravel on a road with a ford across the River Avon. A monastery was established there in the seventh century but it died out quickly before the Vikings arrived. Stratford-upon-Avon and Shipston-on-Stour have Anglo-Saxon names and expanded in size during this period. The Vale of the Red Horse was the name for the valley of the River Stour and attracted Anglo-Saxon settlers as shown by the preponderance of '- ington' place name word endings in that valley. A large group of Anglo-Saxons was based around Bidford-on-Avon and they also had halls at Hatton Rock and Long Itchington. At this time Bidford-on-Avon was the commercial and social centre of its surrounding area rather than nearby Alcester which rose to prominence later.

Anglo-Saxon names in the area of Tanworth-in-Arden indicate that the Ferny Wood in Oldberrow, the White Wood (Monwode Lea) in Arley and the Old Wood (also named Mockley Wood) in Ullenhall existed at this time and still exist today. Kineton was mentioned in a Saxon charter in 969 but there was no mention of a church in the town at this time.

The name of Walton near Wellesbourne indicates that there was also an Anglo-Saxon royal vill in this location. The estate in Shottery was linked to the wooded estate at Nuthurst from the seventh century. Similarly Tanworth-in-Arden was later linked to Brailes in 1086. Researchers have traced a number of tracks which were possibly used to drive animals from Feldon to Arden for the winter. The next nearest large towns to Warwickshire to the south were Hereford, founded in the seventh century, and Worcester which was founded in the ninth century.

It is remarkable that it took several hundred years for Old English, the language of the Angles, to replace the British (Celtic) language but English still survives in a recognisable form today.

Fig 24. Morton Bagot church which has early timber framing inside, although most of the church was built in about 1300 and the bell-tower is from around 1600. It is reputed to be the last candle-lit church in England. The barn on the right is being restored in 2009

Farming

It is likely that the area of land that was being cultivated was reduced because the total population was less when the Romans left and some of the land reverted to woodland. Pollen analysis carried out at the Roman site at Metchley (Edgbaston) shows that the woodland regenerated in post-Roman times as less land was used for cultivation. Even so the vast majority of the historic woodland had gone at this time. One estimate is that in later Anglo Saxon times only 3% of woodland survived in the north west of the county, 2% in the north east and as little as 1% in the south. However there was certainly a large wood to the south west of Warwick in 900 and many other well-wooded areas.

The Anglo-Saxons used primitive ploughs from the fifth century and they introduced to England much better ploughs than had been used previously. Generally across Warwickshire in Saxon times the land was farmed in strips in a 3 or 4 field system. In this open field system there were typically 3 large fields with one of them left fallow each year. They continued to be cultivated in strips and grazed in common. The allocation of strips seems to have been intended to give each family a fair share of land in terms of quantity and quality of land and distance from the settlement. However there is evidence that in some settlements allocations of land were made simply by drawing lots.

The measurement of land at this time was usually based on the amount that could be ploughed with one ox. This varied from place to place. Typical units of measurement which were widely used are -

1 ox (plough) = 1 bovate = 15 acres,

2 ox (plough) = 1 virgate = 30 acres.

1 hide = the land that one ox could plough in a year (1 fallow) = 120 acres.

1 plough team (2 oxen) = 2 hides = 240 acres,

An indication of the cultivated area of the tribal regions is found in the 'Tribal Hidage' which is believed to have been compiled between 750 and 950. This indicates that Mercia (including north Warwickshire) had a total of 30,000 hides and Hwicce (including the south of the county) had just 300 hides. The estimates for Warwickshire alone in the Tribal Hidage are about 1200 hides before 1066 and 1388 hides in a later assessment in the Domesday Book in 1086. This suggests that about 150,000 to 170,000 acres was being cultivated when the total area of Warwickshire was around 600,000 acres.

Although there is no present proof that there were vineyards in Warwickshire in Saxon times it is very likely that there were because there was at least one nearby in Worcestershire. If present these would have been a distinctive feature of the landscape. Management of woodlands was well advanced from early times. Two types of crops were taken from the woodland, underwood and coppice were taken every seven years or so and full grown trees were felled about every 30 years. The felling and clearing of trees led to areas being called 'assarts' from the French word meaning to grub up. The Anglo Saxon charters for Warwickshire show the spread of cultivation and people from Feldon into Arden because there are many charters recording land ownership in the south of the county but few in the north at this time.

Industry, Roads,

In the seventh century the principle of the water wheel was brought into Britain from the Arab world. There is evidence of at least three water mills in south Warwickshire in Saxon times at Alveston, Clifford Chambers and Blackwell. There were also at least 5 salt pans in Warwickshire in Saxon times processing raw materials brought from Droitwich. Although most buildings were made from timber there is evidence of mortared masonry in Warwickshire at this time and therefore there must have been some quarrying taking place. Despite the ready availability of timber and nearby ironstone in Oxfordshire and Northamptonshire there is no remaining evidence of iron workings in Warwickshire in Saxon times. There was a mint in Warwick intermittently from 976.

The existence of a network of roads is apparent from the widespread use of them as landmarks in Anglo Saxon land charters. Road bridges were paid for by some form of taxation from the eighth century. Major through routes were referred to as the King's Way whereas smaller roads were usually termed a Common Way, a Church Way or a Lane.

Control of roads was important for society and an archaic word found in records of offences at this time is 'purpresture' which is the offence of encroaching onto common land which included a road. The roads in Warwickshire in Saxon times continued to be based around the network built by the Romans; that is Fosse Way, Watling Street, Ryknild Street and the Saltways radiating from Droitwich. However it is unlikely that they were always well maintained and there were also many other trackways.

Fig 25. The Saxon sanctuary within Wootton Wawen church

Churches & Religion, Fortifications

Churches form many of the landmarks in the landscape and some information about the history of religious belief will indicate the context in which church-building developed. Saxons were pagans when they arrived in Warwickshire and sites of 30 pagan burials have been identified in the county, probably from the fifth and sixth centuries.

Religious and secular lives were closely interwoven in later Saxon days. Augustine of Canterbury arrived from Rome on the Isle of Thanet in 597 to spread Christianity and from 602 missionaries travelled to spread the gospel throughout the land. This was very effective and Warwickshire was probably wholly Christian by about 685. It is believed that most Christian churches were built on existing sacred sites which had been used from pagan times.

In the Saxon period Warwickshire was split between two dioceses with the southern part in Worcester and the remainder in Lichfield. There is evidence that Hwicce may have converted to Christianity relatively early because the first Christian king in Mercia was crowned in 655. Early Christianity was based on minsters which were initially built of timber but were very soon built of stone. One of the earliest minsters was quite near to Warwickshire at Brixworth in Northamptonshire and was established as early as 600. There was also a bishop in Lichfield from around the same time. The minster at Wootton Wawen was founded around 800 and the existing church was established about 950. A substantial part of the Saxon sanctuary survives within the present church. Many churches were built in the county in the ninth and tenth centuries and most parishes had a church in some form. Many of them were subsequently rebuilt or much modified in the fourteenth and later centuries.

The Benedictine monastery at Coventry was late Anglo Saxon, about 975 to 1044, and Polesworth Abbey was established around the same time. There were also monasteries at Alderminster and Tredington and there were minsters at Inkberrow, Stratford-upon-Avon and Hanbury before 850. There is also a pre-Norman structure at Studley church. At this time there were a number of holy wells such as those at Southam and at St Osburg's pool in Coventry. The Vikings were pagans when they arrived in Britain but also became Christians towards the end of the tenth century.

Chapter Seven

The Normans 1066 to 1300

Introduction

The date of 1066 is well known because it was a crucial year for Britain with the invasion by William the Conqueror who led the Norman (French) contingent which landed near Hastings in that year. Many things in the country would never be the same again. The invaders conquered and subjugated the country quite rapidly although there was some resistance to the Normans in Mercia in our part of the country. This obstacle was overcome by 1070 and many of the existing local lords subsequently lost their land to the Normans because of their association with the resistance. Thereafter Britain came under powerful French influence for the following 600 years. This is the first period about which we know much more about the development of the landscape because there are documentary records beginning with the very substantial and valuable Domesday Book of 1086.

Settlements

Bedworth, Nuneaton, Coleshill, Long Compton and Kineton are listed in the Domesday Book amongst about 208 recorded parishes but Alcester and a number of other places are not mentioned. This is strange because Alcester, for example, was an extensive area running to the north-west of the present town. It may have been because Alcester was a royal manor at the time. Solihull is not mentioned in the Domesday Book but the manors of Ulverlie, Langdone and Elmdone are listed. Nuneaton was a small settlement at this time and there were probably only about forty cottages running along the village street which is now known as Bondgate and Church Street.

Bedworth was listed in the Domesday Book as Bedeworde and had a population of 60 people with an area between 240 and 480 acres in cultivation. The details which were recorded included 4 hides (about 120 acres each), land for 6 ploughs, meadow 16 acres, woodland, 1 league x half league (1 league was about 3 miles), 1 Lord, 5 Villagers, 3 Smallholders and 2 Slaves. Also in Arden, Coleshill still had about 20 square miles (12,800 acres) of woodland and only around 200 acres of land were being cultivated. On the other hand Long Compton in the far south of the county in Feldon had a huge area of around

3600 acres (5.5 square miles) under cultivation in 3 or 4 open fields. Kineton was also well established with a population around 500 and it was the administrative centre of a hundred. The isolated farmsteads in Morton Bagot were established in this time, Netherstead began in the twelfth century, Greenhill Farm is first mentioned in 1262 and it is part timber-framed and Ouerton began in 1290 on the site of Manor Farm. There was a fortified Manor House next to the church in Chesterton and the manor was known as a berwick because the manor house was located in the manor.

Fig 26. Minsters in Warwickshire

Agriculture, Cultivation, Ridge and Furrow,
Fishponds, Dovecotes, Climate

We have seen that the 'champion' land of Feldon had been cultivated for many centuries whereas the higher land of Arden had been more slowly developed and more of it remained as woodland. The name 'Arden' was first documented in the eleventh century; agricultural development began in earnest under the Normans and was well under way in the twelfth century.

Hedgerows are a major feature of the landscape. There is a theory that the age of a hedge can be calculated roughly from the number of species of hedge plants found in thirty yards. The theory, known as Hooper's Rule, suggests that a find of 9 species or more in a 30 yard length indicates a hedge which is 1000 years old.

The economy and the social structure developed and in 1086 it has been estimated that the distribution of income, occupation of land and tenancy was something like that shown in the panel.

Income		Occupiers of Land		Tenants	
Barons	50%	Villeins	40%	Villeins	47%
Church	25%	Landlords	35%	Cottagers	30%
King	15%	Freemen	20%	Freemen	15%
Others	10%	Cottagers	5%	Slaves	8%

In this period cultivation of the land became more intensive and in some areas pasture was in short supply. In many places the small enclosed fields, some dating to Celtic times and generally referred to as Celtic fields, were abandoned and the larger Midland open fields were adopted and ridge and furrow cultivation became the norm. The ridge and furrow system can often still be identified on the ground and frequently has a curve at the end of each furrow where the ox plough was turned – this is called an 'aratral' curve. This curve can also sometimes be seen in the shape of the surviving hedges. A three field system was widely adopted where each year one field was fallow, one was for spring sowing and the other was for autumn sowing. This rotation was found from experience to give superior crop yields. In the Avon valley the open field system was introduced at an early date on the gravel soils which were easier to work. (Examples of open field cultivation still exist at Laxton in Nottinghamshire.). Areas of ridge and furrow are still visible at Kineton, Napton and Arlescote and many other villages. Chesterton had three fields named Open Fields Grett or Conygre field, The Moor and Owe field.

The Domesday Book reveals that in south Warwickshire (Feldon) there were around 1.7 ploughs per square kilometre whereas in Arden the figure was only about one quarter of this. When the Normans arrived the open field system was initially less widespread in Arden but during the next three centuries new farms and fields were made from clearance of wood and waste land in the north of the county. Both Stoneleigh Abbey and Wroxall Nunnery assarted land in this period. Unfortunately it was found that assarting led to erosion and a tendency for land that remained uncultivated to turn to heath-land quite quickly. There was therefore generally a mix of farms and open field cultivation with open fields dominating the south of the county. Later, in the thirteenth century, meadows beside rivers were used for hay and grazing.

In the north-east of the county on the High Cross Plateau farming yields were poor before 1066 but an arable four field system was widely adopted under the Normans and population and production increased. Nuneaton had three immense undivided open fields between the village and Watling Street at this time. Evidence of ridge and furrow can still be seen near Moat Farm at the junction of the A444 & M6. In Nuneaton the farmers in Bond End already had houses in the eleventh century. Meanwhile Bedworth had been cut out of the Forest of Arden but there was still a great deal of woodland remaining. We have noted that Coleshill was largely wooded, especially in the west, until the thirteenth century and there was grazing at Coleshill Heath to the south.

In Alcester there was one very large open field to the south of the parish. The two fields to the north strictly speaking belonged to the village of Kings Coughton. In Alcester and other districts the strips in the fields were called lands or selions.

As manors were developed as the residences of the lords many of them constructed fishponds and dovecotes to extend the range of food which was available to eat. Dovecotes were widespread at this time to provide pigeons for food. Over 40 have been noted in the county. One is preserved by the National Trust at Kinwarton. In addition to the usual food crops hemp was widely grown in Arden and was used especially to make nets.

From 950 to 1300 the climate gradually became warmer and dryer and tender crops, such as grape vines, could be grown in England. The tree-line also became higher at more elevated locations. However from the mid fourteenth century the climate deteriorated again and crop yields were reduced.

Woodland, Forests, Parks

From around the year 700 the woodland was seen as a valuable resource in itself and it was decided that some areas should be retained. Woodland was kept mainly for coppicing and pollarding and the right to cut wood and timber was closely controlled. From the thirteenth century there was also some deliberate preservation of woods in Arden for cropping. Pollarding was used to prevent grazing animals from reaching the growing shoots. The Domesday

Book shows that about 19% of Warwickshire was woodland, mainly in the north. This was less than counties to the west. For example Worcestershire was about 40% woodland. At this time some parishes in the county had as much as 50% woods whereas others were less than 10%. In 1086 the parish of Tanworth-in-Arden was largely woodland. The present Mockley Wood near Tanworth-in-Arden is very old and probably dates back to Norman times. In the far north of the county the High Cross Plateau had lost most of its woodland by 1066.

'Forest' at this time was a word generally reserved for a particular character of woodland which was kept as cover for game. It was not a term used as a simile for a large wood as it is today. From 700 to 1400 Forest Law kept designated land, not just woodland, for hunting by lords of the manor. Forest Law kept the beasts of the forest for the king and his officials and these animals included deer and wild boar. Arden was an extensive forest until 1066 but this reduced quite rapidly after the Normans arrived. Arden was never a Royal forest because it was under the influence of the Earls of Warwick and not the king. A Royal forest was not usually fenced. Norman Kings sold parts of their forests to raise money from around 1250. There is little extensive Norman forest left now and the nearest to the Warwickshire boundary is at Cannock Chase in Staffordshire.

Local lords of the manor established parks for hunting deer from the eighth century and they usually constructed a ditch and bank boundary around the park. In contrast to forest a park was always fenced to keep deer from escaping. Deer parks were very popular in Norman times and a number of new ones were created. From the thirteenth century a licence was required to empark land and licences were also granted for peasants to graze land in parks. Parks were typically about 250 acres in extent. From the twelfth to the fourteenth century many manorial deer parks were established in Arden. At one time there was a total of 52 deer parks in the county.

Most of the medieval parks in the county have now been lost although remnants of later ones survive such as those at Charlecote Park and Packington. Sutton Park was created in 1126 as Sutton Chase and was granted to the Earls of Warwick by Henry I. The present Sutton Park is a partial survivor of the Chase but the trees have been felled although quantities of holly remain. Henry II established a later park at Kenilworth. The story is told of one Thomas Burdet who had a Park at Arrow near Alcester where he had a favourite white buck. He was very upset when Edward IV killed this buck and told the king so. Unfortunately he was convicted of treason for this outburst and he was executed for daring to criticise the monarch.

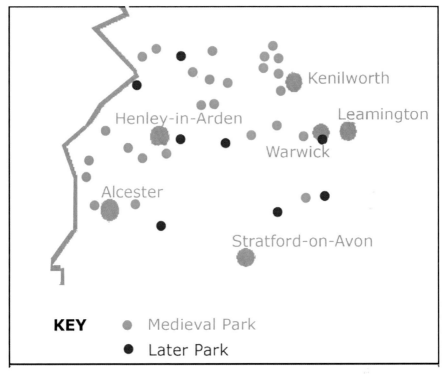

Fig 27. Parks in the Arden Area

Buildings

Many relatively large houses were constructed during these centuries including those listed in Fig 28.

Eleventh Century	
Alspath Hall, Meriden	Longdon Hall, Solihull
Hopsford Hall, Withybrook	Marston Hall, Bickenhill
Kington Grange, Claverdon	Warwick Castle, Warwick

Twelfth Century	
Berwood Hall, Minworth	Cryfield Grange, Stoneleigh
Bode Hall, Tamworth	Kenilworth Castle, Kenilworth
Charlecote,	Whoberley Hall, Stoneleigh
Coombe Abbey,	

Thirteenth Century	
Alscott Hall, Coleshill	Kimberley Hall, Kingsbury
Ashfurlong Hall, Sutton Coldfield	Mercote Hall, Berkswell
Astley Castle, Astley	Millburn Grange, Stoneleigh
Bramcote Hall, Polesworth	Nailcote Hall, Berkswell
Brook House, Ullenhall	Newland Hall, Exhall
Brook House, Ansley	Ouston Grange, Lea Marston
Castle Bromwich Hall, Castle Bromwich	Peddimore Hall, Sheldon
Coton Hall, Hurley	Pirrey Mill, Princethorpe
Duddleston Hall, Aston	Shelford House, Burton Hastings
Grange The, Radway	Walsh Hall, Meriden
Grange The, Solihull	Wedgnock Park, Warwick
Halloughton Hall, Kingsbury	Weston Ho, Long Compton
Hargrave Hall, Bickenhill	Widney Manor, Solihull
Home Grange, Stoneleigh	

Fig 28. Country Houses built in the Norman period

Very few remnants of 'ordinary' or 'vernacular' houses survive from the early Norman period. Peasant houses were simple timber framed structures built with no foundations and had a short life because they soon rotted. There are some examples of 'cruck' cottages remaining where two large curved oak timbers are used to build each of the A-frames between the bays which support the roof but these are difficult to date accurately. Cruck houses can be seen in Stoneleigh, Polesworth, Rowington, Over Whitacre and Monks Kirby. In Upper Spernall it is possible to see some old timber houses which probably date from this time which have been converted to barns.

In the eleventh century the lords lived in manors which were generally large timber framed buildings but more substantial buildings such as churches, castles and some bigger houses were being built with stone. Quarries were dug to provide the stone and these were usually quite close to the building site to reduce the effort of transport. From 1150 to 1350 many manor houses in Arden were built with moats. There were 12 moated farms in Tanworth-in-Arden alone. The larger moated houses include Baddesley Clinton, Coughton Court and Morton Bagot. The provision of moats appears to have been a matter of style or fashion rather than practicality. The same goes for the choice between timber, brick or stone for the construction of houses because, although there is some correlation between the materials used and the availability of them, it does appear that again style and fashion were very influential amongst wealthier people.

Many of these fortified and moated manor houses were built and villages often grew up around them. Some of the earliest were Ingon Grange at Hampton Lucy, Alspath Hall at Meriden, Hopsford Hall at Withybrook, Kington Grange at Claverdon, Longdon Hall at Solihull and Marston Hall at Bickenhill. Others were Whoberley Hall at Stoneleigh, Charlecote House, Cryfield Grange at Stoneleigh, Berwood Hall at Minworth, Bode Hall at Tamworth, and Coombe Abbey near Brinklow.

Castles and other fortifications were built during the first century of Norman occupation as symbols of power. Coventry Castle was built at this time along with the defensive ditches in the city known as Hyrsum and Red Ditch. Unfortunately no trace of the castle remains. The castle at Warwick was rebuilt in substantial style in 1068. Many agree that the view of Warwick Castle from the main road bridge over the River Avon must be one of the best views in Warwickshire, if not in England.

Fig 29. The Motte and Bailey at Brinklow.
This area has recently been cleared by the local parish council

Henley-in-Arden was established in 1141 and a castle was built at Beaudesert – the huge mound still survives. Kenilworth Castle was built in the twelfth century and other castles were built at Studley and Aston Cantlow. King John's Mound motte and bailey was constructed in Kineton about 1216 to the south of Warwick Road. There is a Norman motte and bailey at Mancetter, east of Hayes Wood and another at Seckington which is 30 feet high. Brinklow 'tump' was originally an earlier burial ground and became Bryncon motte and bailey from 1135 and it is one of the best of its type in the country. Many bridges were also built at this time and there is an ancient stone bridge at Hunningham.

Fig 30. Warwick Castle, showing the main East Gate and Guy's Tower

Deserted Villages

When religious houses first established their lands the existing settlements were often cleared away and the residents were displaced. This led to a number of deserted villages in Warwickshire. For example the building of Coombe Abbey was responsible for the destruction of the two hamlets of Upper and Lower Smite and similarly the construction of Stoneleigh Abbey led to the loss of the village of Cryfield in the twelfth century when the Cistercians arrived.

In later years there were a number of other reasons for deserted villages including plague, the establishment of new forests, the later enclosures and the creation of parks from the fourteenth to nineteenth centuries. However

Newbold Pacey was enclosed early on, in 1327, when the hovels were pulled down and the people were moved to Ashorne.

Hundreds

Counties in the West Midlands were usually divided into sub-divisions called hundreds. The ten hundreds in Warwickshire at the time of the Domesday Book are described in Fig 31.

1. Coleshill hundred, named for the town, and later renamed Hemlingford from a ford over the Tame near Kingsbury, probably included the old hundreds of Tamworth, Birmingham, Solihull and Atherstone.

2. Bomelau (a place not now identifiable near Brandon) later became part of Knightlow hundred, named for a hill on Dunsmore Heath.

3. Meretone hundred, named for Marton, later became part of Knightlow hundred.

4. Stanlei hundred, named for Stoneleigh, later became part of Knightlow hundred.

5. Tremelau hundred, may have been named after a hill near Lighthorne church, later became part of Kineton hundred.

6. Honesberie hundred, place not identified although there is a farm of this name near Priors Marston, later became part of Kineton hundred.

7. Fexhole hundred, place not identified, later became part of Kineton hundred.

8. Berricestone hundred, named for Barcheston, later became part of Kineton hundred.

9. Fernecumbe hundred, place not identified, later became part of Barlichway hundred, named for land on a hill between Haselor and Burton.

10. Patelau hundred, later Pathlow, named for a mound between Stratford and Wootton Wawen, later became part of Barlichway hundred.

Fig 31. Warwickshire hundreds in 1086

There may also have been an eleventh hundred at Coton (now Coten End) near Warwick but this is uncertain. These ten hundreds were reorganised into four in the twelfth century. As mentioned in the panel they are Hemlingford, Knightlow, Kineton and Barlichway hundreds.

Industry & Commerce

A large proportion of the population spent most of their time cultivating the land but many of them turned their hands to other work from time to time. As the years went by people began to specialise in particular work and what we now call industry developed. Early industries included forging of iron by the blacksmith, woodworking by the carpenter and the making of cooking and eating utensils and tiles from pottery.

Fig 32. Some mills from Norman times onwards

At this time water mills were becoming widespread on nearly every river in the county and and ever more mills were required. Windmills were introduced into Britain in 1191. For example there were two windmills and two watermills

64

in Kineton in 1279, there was a watermill in Nuneaton where Wash Brook joined the river and there were two watermills in Coleshill by 1273.

We have seen that various places specialised in making particular things. For example, by 1150 there were more than a dozen textile mills built in Coventry for the production of wool cloth and the main business of the city was wool weaving from the thirteenth to the seventeenth century. 'Coventry Blue' cloth was famous for its quality over a wide area of the country.

Coal had been dug from near the land surface from late medieval times and the east Warwickshire coalfield was mined from the thirteenth century. This coalfield has steeply sloping seams which descend generally to the south. Bedworth was well known for the production of coal at this time as coal was discovered there before 1275.

In Alcester there is still a Bleachfield Street which is in an area which was noted for the bleaching of linen and this indicates that hemp was grown in the area. Clay was dug to make bricks and this left many ponds on the edges of settlements and sometimes on the village green. Quarries were also created for the getting of stone.

There is some thin evidence that the monks at Bordesley Abbey introduced the needle-making to Alcester at this time.

Markets

Markets became important as the population grew and as people traded surplus food and other goods and manufacturing developed. Markets were licensed by the twelfth century and the local lord of the manor would often start a market in order to generate income from the licence. For example, Henley-in-Arden market was established in 1220 and Kineton received its market charter in 1227. We have noted that Nuneaton received a charter for a market in the thirteenth century and Brinklow was a market town from 1218 until about 1818.

Population and Disease

There was a rapid rise in population under the Normans but there were also some large fluctuations caused by outbreaks of deadly diseases. In the mid and later Norman period Britain was beset by a number of bouts of disease. There is more detail in the next chapter. These epidemics greatly reduced the population and the use of the land for agriculture. There would be further waves of disease in the fifteenth and sixteenth centuries.

One estimate is that the population of England in 1066 was around 1.25 million. However another estimate is that the population of England as a whole was between 1.75 million to 2.25 million. In 1086 the rural population of Warwickshire can be calculated from the Domesday Book to be around 5 to 10 people per square mile in the south (Feldon) but much less at 2 to 5 to the square mile in the north (Arden). This suggests a total rural population between 2,500 and 6,000. If the whole population of England was spread out evenly across the country then there would have been about 20,000 people in Warwickshire. It is therefore clear that Warwickshire was not one of the most densely populated areas when the Normans arrived. However the population increased steadily until 1300 and woodland continued to be felled to provide land for cultivation. In Feldon in the twelfth and thirteenth century the population was becoming too great for the resources of the countryside and some people migrated to the towns. In Arden the parishes of Tanworth-in-Arden and Stoneleigh both had an increase of around 300% in population from 1086 to 1250.

Fig 33. Norman church doorway at Beaudesert

Religion, Monastic Houses, Schools

During the Norman period many religious buildings were constructed, land was often taken over by a monastery, an abbey or a priory and the resident villagers moved away. From 1066 churches were usually built from stone and there were 254 medieval churches in Warwickshire by the early thirteenth century.

Before the Normans arrived ecclesiastical centres were usually based on minsters and from 900 to 1300 churches were usually built adjacent to the local noblemen's houses and not at the centre of a village. The local lord built the church and collected a tithe of 10%. Tithe barns were built from the middle ages to store the grain and other materials given to the lord as tithes. Granges were run as farms to provide food for monasteries and abbeys and, for example, Merevale Abbey had a grange. Nowadays the name 'grange' is often used simply to signify a big house.

Fig 34. The south side of Warwick Castle, the classic view from Avon bridge

When the Normans arrived in Warwickshire the administration of the church was mainly based in Worcester and it had vast estates in Warwickshire. There was also an ecclesiastical centre nearby at Lichfield which moved to Chester in 1075 and then back south to Coventry in 1102 and this occupied some estates in the north of the county.

In Nuneaton land at Attleborough and Stockingford was taken for the use of a Priory in the twelfth century and this priory had 93 nuns in 1234. The Priory established housing on Abbey Street in the town in the thirteenth century and around the same time it obtained a charter for a market which continues to this day. A new market place was constructed to the west of the River Anker in the thirteenth century.

Alcester Abbey was founded in 1138; it was always small and was soon demoted to the status of a Priory. A lane known as Birch Abbey and a street called Priory Road still exist in the town.

In the twelfth and thirteenth centuries over twenty monasteries, abbeys and priories were established in the county and most of them took land and cleared it for keeping sheep. Further details are in Fig 35. It is believed that Coombe Abbey alone kept 20,000 sheep at the end of the thirteenth century. The word abbey is the general term for a monastic house whereas a monastery is for men who live under an abbot, a convent is for women under an abbess, a priory is under a prior or prioress and a nunnery is a convent of nuns.

The impact of the new buildings and the changes in agriculture and settlements had a profound, if gradual, effect on the landscape. Traces of many of these establishments can still be found. The Benedictine house at Alvecote was established in 1159 and has a Norman doorway and Wroxall was a Benedictine nunnery established in 1141 and part of it remains as a church known as the Wren church.

There were Benedictine monasteries at -

Coventry Abbey or Priory (founded in 1043).

Alcester (founded in1138), little now remains.

Alvecote Priory (founded 1159), fragments of walls remain.

Nuneaton Nunnery, parts survive, twelfth century.

Henwood Priory, Solihull, 1149 to 1161.

Wroxall Abbey, founded as a Priory in 1141, most pulled down in 1560.

Polesworth Abbey which survives as a church, founded ninth century, church and gatehouse remain.

There were Cistercian abbeys were at -

Coombe (Coventry), established in the period 1124 to 1154, now a hotel, much of the original abbey was demolished to build a grand house, originally the Abbey of Cumbe, cloisters still exist.

Merevale, founded 1148, gate chapel remains as a parish church, other substantial stonework remains.

Stoneleigh, founded 1154, gatehouse remains, another grand house has taken the name.

Bordesley, founded 1138, near Redditch, ruins are visible.

Pinley Priory, near Claverdon, no remains.

There were Carthusian establishments at

St Annes Priory in Coventry was founded much later in 1381.

There were Augustinian priories at

Maxstoke Priory, founded 1336, ruins now next to church.

Kenilworth Abbey and Priory of St Mary founded 1123 to 1129, substantial ruins remain.

Wootton Wawen Priory, about 1178.

Studley Priory, Priory Farm includes a few fragments.

Alcester, there is a Priory Road.

Arbury Priory, Chilvers Coton, established in the period 1154 to 1189.

There were Dominican friars (the Blackfriars) were established at Warwick before 1263.

Temple Balsall (Knights Templars), the Preceptory or Old Hall survives in a Victorian outer brick coat. From 1100 the Knights Templars grew in power but they were disbanded in 1312. Temple Herdewyke, Temple Balsall and Temple Grafton were all owned by the Knights Templars. In Temple Herdewyke the chapel survives but looks like a barn and the church at Temple Balsall survives.

The earlier Atherstone abbey was dedicated to St Mary. It was established by Austin Friars before 1086. St Mary's chapel is on the site, an old tower and chancel were retained.

Atherstone abbey was dedicated to St Scholastica, it was founded in 1859. The ruins of the earlier friary can still be seen near the surviving abbey building.

Benedictine, Atherstone nunnery order of Blessed Sacrament.

There were also Carmelite friars at Coventry before 1300.

Fig 35. Some of the monastic establishments in Warwickshire

The churches built in the Norman period include Seckington, 1150; Austrey, which has a thirteenth century Early English tower; Lapworth, a fine church from 1100 with a fifteenth century spire; Morton Bagot, the earliest part is thirteenth century and it is built on a natural Arden sandstone bluff from Lias limestone with sandstone details. Baddesley Clinton, thirteenth century with a fifteenth century tower; Rowington has a twelfth century tower which is unusually at the east end of the church. Haselor is an isolated little church with a Norman tower and Chesterton church was founded in the eleventh century and is in Perpendicular style and it is built of limestone and Northampton stone.

Henry VIII split England from the Roman Catholic Church in 1534 and, through his chief minister, Thomas Cromwell, dissolved the monasteries in the next few years and many were destroyed. The new owners often built houses for themselves on the site. Arbury Priory was built near Nuneaton around 1198 and later became Arbury Hall which is now occasionally open to the public.

In 1185 the Knights Templar had a manor house south west of Bermuda near Nuneaton. Bermuda was named for the landowner who was governor of the island of Bermuda. In the Avon Valley the town of Stratford-upon-Avon was founded by the Bishop of Worcester in the late twelfth century. The public school at Warwick was definitely in existence by 1123 but some sources say that it dates back as far as 914.

Fig 36. Norman church doorway at St Nicholas, Kenilworth

Settlements, Feldon, Arden, Avon Valley

In 1086 most of today's villages existed in some form in the county. Most parish boundaries were defined in late Saxon charters but many were changed because a number of estates were redistributed by the Normans and the development of villages was often planned to fit in with the needs of the new local landlords. The lands held by the lords were referred to as 'demesnes'. King Edward held four demesnes in Warwickshire and the Leofric family held at least eleven. In 1066 about half of the villages in Warwickshire had their own manor and the others were split between manors. Although some land was held in common before 1066 the term 'common land' was not recorded until the arrival of the Normans.

It has been estimated that 10% of people lived in towns in the eleventh century but this had increased to 20% by the thirteenth century. The number of hides (each equal to about 120 acres) in cultivation in Warwickshire before 1066 was around 1200 but this had increased to 1388 in 1086 when the Domesday Book was compiled.

Agriculture in Feldon was well developed by the Saxons and Vikings before the arrival of the Normans. Compared to Arden there is little evidence of significant changes and development in Feldon during the Norman period. As we have seen the Feldon area became developed before the Arden area and village clusters were forming in the ninth and tenth centuries and becoming larger by 1200. Before this time the settlements are more accurately described as hamlets. Feldon was relatively prosperous by 1066 although some parts, such as Shuckburgh and Flecknoe, remained somewhat mysterious and empty.

The colonisation of Arden developed as spare land to the south of the county in Feldon became scarce and development was encouraged by lords of the manor who wanted to see their holdings grow in value and so new farmsteads were established. Newton Regis is named from Henry II because it became a Royal Manor in his reign in 1159.

The development of Coventry was encouraged by a charter in 1150 which promised a tax-free year for anyone who built property in the town. So successful was this and other incentives that Coventry became the fourth largest town in England by the end of the fourteenth century. Construction of the town wall was begun in 1350. Following two centuries of growth Coventry fell into decline as the powerful guilds banded together to discourage newcomers.

Other towns in the county also experienced expansion at this time. Bedworth was large enough to be listed in the Domesday Book, Nuneaton was well established by the twelfth century, Kenilworth grew in size around 1140 and Rugby was granted a charter for a market in 1255. In 1140 Thurston de Montfort built Beaudesert Castle and obtained a charter for a market in Henley-in-Arden and the current market town was planned and laid out in 1185 on the Stratford to Birmingham road and it became a borough in 1296.

Tanworth-in-Arden is not mentioned in the Domesday Book although some adjoining villages were named. Land in Tanworth was let from 1150 to 1350 further and further from the centre of the village and the demesne land was cleared before 1180. In 1180 the Earl of Warwick created Monkspath to the north of the village. There was significant growth in population in Tanworth in the late thirteenth century and from 1250 to 1340 there was yet another third phase of development. Over a long period Tanworth had a close link with Brailes in Feldon to the south.

Warwick existed as an important burgh and shire town in the eleventh century and in 1080 the population was between 1000 and 2000. Stratford-on-Avon grew rapidly from 1182 to 1252. About 1185 Alcester was created at the crossing of Ryknild Street and the Roman road from Stratford. In 1230 there were tenants in Leamington Priors, the original name for the town now known as Royal Leamington Spa, together with a watermill and 100 acres.

Fig 37. Clopton Bridge at Stratford-on-Avon. This bridge carries
heavy traffic although it was last rebuilt in 1480

Transport

Norman roads were very poor because the Roman roads had deteriorated and there was no system for ensuring maintenance or building of them. However roads were in use for long journeys to transport salt from Droitwich and wool from monastic and other estates for export. There is a Salt Street in No Mans Heath denoting that it was used to transport salt for a long time.

In Coleshill it has been noted that road maintenance was carried out under the Statute of Winchester of 1285 to remove bushes and other hiding places where men with evil intent may lurk. Some of the Holloways in Arden are reckoned to be over 1,000 years old.

Chapter Eight

Fourteenth Century

Prosperity for Some, Food for Most, Poverty for Many to Come,
Early Enclosures, Feldon, More Assarting in Arden

Agriculture reached a height of productivity in the early fourteenth century and most of the population had an adequate food supply. However there were a number of influences during the century which would mitigate against further growth in production including climate change and a fall in the labour supply. There was also an intermittent and far-reaching process of reorganisation of agriculture over the next few centuries.

Fig 38. Cruck cottage at Polesworth. The curved
sloping timbers originally supported the roof

The way in which agriculture was organised in England changed radically from around this time. Beginning in about 1350 the enclosure of land began in various parts of England in a piecemeal, informal way and over four or five centuries the open field system of large fields was replaced throughout most of the country by a patchwork of smaller fields which was the basis of much of the countryside we see today. However this process of Enclosure did not begin in Warwickshire until later on in the sixteenth century.

Fig 39. Maxstoke Castle is a fine example of a moated manor house in Arden

Some villages in Feldon continued with the open field system until a much later date in the nineteenth century. There was a two field system in south Warwickshire until the fourteenth or fifteenth centuries at many villages including Hampton Lucy, Harbury, Ladbroke, Brailes, Tysoe, Ettington, Tredington and Stratford-upon-Avon. Aston Cantlow also had a two field arrangement in 1273 but this had evolved into a three field regime by 1348 and later a four, or even a five field, system was used.

In Coleshill in 1300 there were three large open fields called Parkfield, Blythfield and Grimshillfield and these made up a total of 900 acres (1.4 square miles). There were also smaller open field systems nearby at Gilson, Hawkswell, Kingshurst and Allcot. In the fourteenth century in Coleshill the population was outgrowing the supply of food and more marginal land was brought into cultivation. This process was accelerated by disastrous crop yields in 1315.

Long Lawford was using a two field system in the thirteenth century and a three field system in the next century. Tanworth-in-Arden was much later in developing and had only about 10% of the area of land cultivated on an open three field system. The remainder of the land was cultivated in many small fields which had been cut from the woodland in a piecemeal fashion.

Woodland, Grassland, Ponds

Woodland was still being cleared in Arden in this century. The bulk of the settlement of Bedworth was cut out of The Forest of Arden around this time but there was still a great deal of woodland remaining throughout north Warwickshire. Despite the constant reference to the tilling of the land and the variety of open field systems in use it is important to remember that grassland was also an important part of the food production system. Grassland was used for a number of purposes. 'Meadow' was mown for hay and 'pasture' was used for grazing by farm animals. Pasture takes some years to establish and therefore is not ploughed up without serious consideration. On the other hand 'natural' grassland grows where trees cannot grow because it is either too dry or too cold. Place names derived from the use of land for pasture include mead, ley, ham, leaze and leasowe. Rabbits were introduced to England in the Middle Ages.

Ponds were very common at this time and it has been estimated that there were nearly six ponds per square mile throughout England and Wales. Ponds were created by a wide range of causes including landslips, dells, charcoal pits, moats, dams, fishponds, dewponds, marlpits, claypits, brickpits, quarries, mines, bellpits, drifts and flashes. It is sometimes difficult to discern the origin of water features but the largest in the county at Kingsbury Water Park are clearly based on flooded gravel pits.

Moated Houses, Growth of Coventry, Black Death,
The Class System Emerges, Market Towns.

We have seen that Warwickshire has a concentration of houses surrounded by moats, especially in the Arden area, and many of these continued to be built in the fourteenth century. Buildings at this time began to become more substantial and generally used local materials. Construction of other structures, such as bridges and churches, also continued. However general housing continued to be less substantial and often only had a life of 20 to 30 years before being rebuilt.

Coventry had grown to be by far the biggest town in the county by this time having been documented as a settlement from 1043. Elsewhere a bridge was built across the River Cole at Coleshill in or before 1360 and the church in the town was built in 1340. Church building styles at this time were Early English or Decorated style from 1250 to 1350 and the Perpendicular style from the mid fourteenth century.

In 1393 King Richard II passed an Act making it compulsory for public houses and inns to have a sign in order to identify them to the official Ale

Taster. The king's own emblem is the 'White Hart' which was first used in London. There are White Hart public houses at Newbold-on-Stour and Ufton.

From the middle of the eleventh century the population of Britain increased by about 50% each century until the negative impact of the Black Death in the middle of the fourteenth century. The population of Coventry alone at this time was between 5,000 and 10,000. The number of people tended to increase with the ability of the land to produce food for them. There were great fluctuations of fortunes in this century and there was a serious decline in agriculture in 1307 and this was followed by a great famine in 1315. Problems were caused by the use of much of the land for sheep rearing instead of cultivation and in 1337 the export of wool was prohibited.

Fig 40. Tysoe Church is Norman with fourteenth century additions

Much the most serious set-back was the Black Death in 1348-9 and this dealt a heavy blow to the manorial system, many demesne lands were let and much land laid down to grass instead of active cultivation. 250 people were killed by the disease in the village of Wappenbury alone and it was abandoned in 1349. Also the village of Chesterton suffered from the plague and was abandoned in 1348. It is believed that rats from Asia brought the fleas which spread the disease all over Europe. The source of the infection in Britain has been traced to Bristol docks. The population of Britain fell catastrophically after the plague from about six million to 2.5 million. There were further plagues in the period from 1360 to 1362, in 1369 and in 1375 and there were a further 13 major outbreaks in the next 100 years. Almost everyone in Bedworth died from the plague in 1349 and the death toll was high throughout the county. In another example Brookhampton near Kineton was totally depopulated by the Black Death in the middle of the fourteenth century. Because of the plague Shustoke near Coleshill moved by about one mile from the old village which had been clustered around the church.

Some consequences of the outbreaks of the plague were that there was a general shortage of labour and wages increased. In 1351 a Statute of Labourers was voted in by Parliament in response to the shortage of labour. Under this statute wages were frozen at a very low level which caused serious hardship for many people. In 1360 the export of corn was forbidden but Richard II allowed export again under certain conditions from 1393. In 1381 there was the Peasants' or Villeins' revolt led by Wat Tyler who rebelled against so many unfair practices of taxation by the manor and the church and the poll tax. The revolt began in Essex in May and spread throughout Kent and Eastern England but the only result of the revolt was the withdrawal of the poll tax.

The social structure of England continued to have the Monarch and the Lords at the top with further layers of Gentry and Yeomen between them and the Peasants. Villagers were able to buy or lease land from the lord of the manor and to become yeomen. The Class System, under which we still live, came about partly because of the growth of a money economy, with the development of medieval trade, commerce, and industry, and partly because of the many peasants' revolts between 1350–1550, especially the keynote 'Peasants' Revolt' of 1381. However villeinage, or serfdom, did not end completely in England until the 16th century. The right for a town to hold a market for the exchange of goods was very valuable for the prosperity of the people. Migration from Feldon into the Arden area continued over a long period from the twelfth century to fourteenth century.

Village Desertion, Climate Change, Windmills, Industrial Development, Roads.

Settlements of different sizes have probably been established and abandoned successively for as long as man has lived in groups. The Warwickshire Time Trail website lists 241 deserted village sites, some of which do not have surviving names. Even so this record does not include the parts of traditional Warwickshire which are now in the area of the West Midlands. Villages were abandoned or greatly depopulated soon after the first outbreak of the plague in 1348 when people fled because of the terror of catching the disease. People also moved away as there was not enough work to earn a living.

Around 3,000 villages were totally deserted in Britain at this time and larger settlements and towns were also left with many abandoned houses.

There were a number of villages largely abandoned in the Feldon area because of the plague including Burton Dassett Southend, Temple Hardwick, Knightcote, Kinwarton, Spernal, Burnells Broom, Wyke and Billesley. It was also necessary to convert large areas of open fields to pasture to accommodate surplus cattle moving from the London area and more sheep were acquired to produce wool. Against the general trend Southam became quite large and important in the fourteenth century.

Fig 41. The bridge over the River Cole at Coleshill built in 1360

Later in this and the following century the cause of further desertion of settlements was usually climate change as crops failed. The period from the thirteenth century to the seventeenth century was a mini Ice Age which affected the ability of the land to produce crops in the same quantities that had led to population expansion and from 1315 to 1317 there was a serious famine.

There was a spate of windmill building from 1180 to 1350 and post mills were in place at Burton Dassett, Avon Dassett, Marton, Shrewley Common, Stockton, Upton and Warmington. There are surviving remains of windmills at Packwood, Rowington Green, Tainters Hill (Kenilworth), Thurlaston, Kineton, Southam, Harbury, Norton Lindsey, Napton, Chesterton, Compton Wynyates (Tysoe) and Berkswell. The windmill from Danzey Green in Warwickshire has been re-erected at the Avoncroft Museum near Bromsgrove in Worcestershire.

Around 1350 in the Bedworth area the random digging of coal holes at Coton and Collycroft was a nuisance to residents and to the cultivation of the land. This fairly random getting of coal was to develop into a major industry in this area in later years. Industry was also developing apace in Coventry. As noted earlier the city was well known for weaving 'Coventry Blue' cloth. The city was also renowned for metal working from the Middle Ages and used ores extracted from the surrounding countryside.

Alcester was a centre for bleaching linen and there is still a Bleachfield Street in the town. The woollen industry also developed as water driven fulling mills were constructed. There were many trades operating in settlements such as Coleshill and Alcester in the fourteenth century.

Brick was becoming a common building material and the number of clay pits multiplied. Brick-built houses lasted longer than the timber framed predecessors and, as we have seen, the brick pits often left ponds when they were abandoned.

The map by Gough of about 1360 records the main roads in the country and shows four or five routes passed through the county of Warwickshire. Feature of the roads at this time were the 'trenches' which were clearings created alongside roads so that highwaymen had no place to hide.

Aylesbury House, Packwood	Lowkes House, Wolfhamcote
Baddesley Clinton	Maxstoke Castle, Maxstoke
Baginton Hall, Baginton	Middleton Hall, Middleton
Broom Hall, Lapworth	Mill House, Church Lawford
Bushwood Hall, Lapworth	Mill House, Lapworth
Caludon Castle, Coventry	New Hall, Sutton Coldfield
East Hall, Sheldon	Rouncil Towers, Kenilworth
Flanders Hall, Kingsbury	Rowley House, Stratford
Grove Park, Warwick	Stoneleigh Abbey, Stoneleigh
Holt Hall, Over Whitacre	Whar Hall, Elmdon
Langley Hall, Solihull	Whateley Hall, Castle Bromwich
Langley Hall, Sutton Coldfield	Wood End Hall, Aston
Leicester Grange, Wolvey	

Fig 42. Major Houses Built in the Fourteenth Century

Chapter Nine

Fifteenth Century

Fig 43. The "Old Forge" at Claverdon

Enclosures beginning in Warwickshire,
Growth of Coventry

In this century the basic system of cultivation was still largely based on the open field system although some villages in the county were planning to adopt the new system of enclosure. Areas which were enclosed in this century included Merevale, Arbury and Berkswell. Enclosure continued, particularly towards the end of the century, as more of the land was converted to pasture, mainly for sheep rearing. In Coleshill parish in the mid-fifteenth century there were many flocks of sheep and most fields were enclosed and some of the present day hedges probably date from this time. In 1432 the village of Chesterton was laid waste because so many of its men were away at war and there were still only eight families in the village in 1509 when the village was enclosed. Following enclosure many peasant families lost income as men were unable to find work because there was less land to cultivate. There was a common rhyme from the time of the enclosures which referred to this new poverty,

"Hark, hark, the dogs do bark, the beggars are coming to town"

Fig 44. Polesworth Abbey, now the parish church for the village

The manorial system was still widespread at this time and some land was taken by lords of the manor to be used as parks particularly in Arden. There was also a concentration of land into larger farms. As noted in the previous chapter, the lack of labour because of disease contributed to making sheep farming more popular. In addition to the formally recognised system of agriculture there were also squatter settlements on the edges of commons in Arden. There was still plenty of wild land and at least eight place names in Warwickshire refer to heath or broom. Because of hardship caused to labourers by the import of cheap corn in 1463 the import of wheat at a price less than 6s.8d, rye less than 4s. and barley less than 3s. per quarter was prohibited.

Coventry was of increasing importance in this century. Henry IV called parliament to meet at Coventry Priory in 1404 but because no lawyers were present at the meeting it became known as the 'Unlearned Parliament'.

Coventry was made a county by Henry VI in 1451. At this time the county of Coventry included the settlements of Whoberley, Biggin, Stoke, Wyken, Caludon, Sowe/Walsgrave (part), Ansty, Radford, Keresley, Harnell, Foleshill, Pinley, Whitley, Styvechale, Exhall, Wood End, Asthill and Horwell. The country as a whole was still divided into regions based on the old Anglo-Saxon Kingdoms and Coventry was the capital of Mercia. The town wall of Coventry was finished around 1400 and had a total length of 2.5 miles; there were twelve gates, of which five were main gates, and between 20 and 32 defensive towers.

The Wars of the Roses, which continued through the years 1450 to 1485, resulted in discontent and disruption throughout much of England from which Warwickshire did not escape. Crops were often trampled by troops on the move, left unplanted or not harvested because it was unsafe or because of lack of labour because men were away as soldiers.

Fig 45. Preston Bagot, a church which has not received a nineteenth century tower

Deserted Villages, Country Houses, Roads.

Yet more villages were deserted during this century and up to as late as 1550. There were as many as 113 villages which were abandoned in south Warwickshire in the thirty five years from 1450 to 1485 alone and they included many in Feldon such as Chesterton and Wormleighton. There were also deserted villages at Fulbrook, Compton Verney, Kingston (now part of

Chesterton), Hatton-on-Avon, Chesterton, Compton Scorpion, Barcheston, Burton Dassett, Whitchurch, Compton Wynyates and Charlecote. Many further people were displaced from their land for the grazing of sheep around 1495.

At least thirteen country houses were constructed in this century including Coughton Court (now National Trust), Birchley Hall at Fillongley, Grove House at Corley, Park House at Stoneleigh, Smorel House at Brailes, Malvern Hall at Solihull, Tocil House at Stoneleigh, Crow Hall at Kingsbury, Elliotts Hall at Tanworth-in-Arden, Marlbrook Hall at Meriden, Salford Hall at Abbots Salford, Treaford Hall at Aston and Walford Hall at Hampton-in-Arden. These all took parcels of land from the countryside into their boundaries.

Ardens Grafton had a quarry which produced very high quality stone from the fifteenth to the nineteenth century. The fifteenth century was also the high point for building churches and, of course, many of them survive today, albeit often much altered during the passing centuries. Beaudesert church tower was built in 1448. The Fish Inn at Wixford is named in memory of the fishponds of monks who came from Evesham. Clopton bridge was built across the Avon at Stratford-upon-Avon in this century and it is still used today by heavy traffic.

Chapter Ten

Sixteenth Century

**Enclosure Continues, More Deserted Villages,
Books on Husbandry, Deer Parks, Potatoes**

This was another century in which developments in agriculture continued apace. Most of the land of Warwickshire still continued to be farmed using the open field system at the start of this century and because of Black Death and other diseases in the previous century there was still a shortage of labour and, of course, reduced demand for food.

Fig 46. The ruins of Kenilworth Castle

The three-field Midland system of land management was generally used only in 'champion' areas such as Feldon. There were four fairly universal characteristics of the Midland open field system. First, the arable land and the meadows were divided into strips; second, arable and meadow land were opened up to pasture after the harvest; third, there was, in addition, common

84

pasture on waste land with the right to gather turf and timber; fourth, the management of all land was subject to direction by the manorial court.

The two main influences on the landscape during the century were the gradual process of enclosure and a trend for landowners to surround their houses with parkland, particularly after 1550. As already noted enclosure took place over a long period. First it was by agreement by the manorial court and later under Parliamentary statute but enclosure in this century was mainly by agreement. The earliest enclosures were often long, narrow fields created by the consolidation of strips. Much of the cultivated land in Feldon was taken over for grazing of sheep at the time of enclosure but some plots of land were marked out to be used as allotments. In Long Compton the area of Weston was enclosed in 1510 for sheep farming. Priors Hardwick was enclosed at the end of the sixteenth century.

Enclosures in south Warwickshire during the Tudor period led to more separate farmsteads and a significant number of empty, deserted villages. Wolfhamcote and Braunstonbury became deserted following enclosure in 1501. Newly created boundary markers were introduced as fields were enclosed and there was a wide variety of types of hedges planted and fences and walls built in Warwickshire at this time. In Feldon in particular there were large geometric fields and a nucleated settlement pattern of small rural villages.

There continued to be distinct differences between the Arden and Feldon areas. In 1540 John Leland wrote in his diaries on one of his tours around England that –

"...the ground in Arden is muche enclosyd, plentifull of gres (grass), but no great plenty of corne. The other part of Warwykshire that lyeth on the left hond or ripe of Avon river, muche to the southe, is for the moste parte champion, somewhat barren of wood, but very plentifull of corne."

During this period, in England as a whole, it is estimated that about 20 million of 37 million acres of usable land remained held in common and was subject to the open field system. Agriculture was becoming more scientific and a number of books were written at this time about how to make use of the land most productively. In 1523 Fitzherbert published 'The Booke of Husbandry', in 1557 Thomas Tusser wrote 'Five Hundred Points of Good Husbandry' and later in 1652 Walter Blith wrote 'The English Improver Improved'. At this time a further factor in the increase of agricultural output was the improvement in agricultural tools such as ploughs.

From 1520 to 1590 grain prices fluctuated wildly up to 100% above and 40% below the average and this greatly affected the stability of farming in Warwickshire, especially in Feldon.

Some sources state that potatoes were introduced to Britain in 1586 when, on 3rd December, Sir Thomas Herriot brought them from Colombia in South America on one of Sir Walter Raleigh's ships. Other sources claim that Sir Walter Raleigh introduced them by way of his estates in Ireland in 1587. However they were brought to Spain somewhat earlier in about 1570. However they did not become a main crop in England until nearly two centuries later, in the 1780s.

As briefly noted earlier it became fashionable to fence large parcels of land to create parks around houses. Manor houses were often built outside a village with a park around them. The parks sometimes had French, Italian and Dutch designs. Warwick and Kenilworth castle deer parks were enclosed from the sixteenth to eighteenth centuries. The garden at Kenilworth Castle has been restored in 2009 to an Elizabethan design.

In Sutton Coldfield the land was so poor that some of the poor sandy soil was taken from the common land for cultivation for a limited period of about five years. In the vicinity of Alcester the production of sheep led to a number of related cottage industries; the area was also known for cattle which were bred for meat and hides and there was a cattle market in Birmingham from Tudor times. Further variety of diet was provided by pillow mounds which were constructed for the rearing of rabbits from the Middle Ages to the sixteenth century.

Population Growth, Kett's Rebellion, Schools, Growth of Industry

In 1538 registers of births, marriages and deaths became compulsory and statistics about the population became much more reliable. In this century the population grew again after the devastation of the plagues in the previous century and more of the land was again under the plough. The population of Britain rose to about 4 million. A few new hamlets and villages were created in Warwickshire and some parts of the county had 10 people per square mile. A general rise in prices and rents began in 1540.

Kett's rebellion in Norfolk began in 1549 and was the last attempt of the English peasant to obtain a fair deal by force. During the campaign Kett made 29 demands from the King which included the end of enclosures and limits on the powers of lords to use common land. However the rebellion failed and about 4,000 people died in the dispute.

In 1508 Bedworth had a population of only about 70 people and it was unfortunately described as 'a most depressing place'. There was a strong rivalry between Bedworth and Collycroft which were then quite separate. The Tudor population of Nuneaton was about 900.

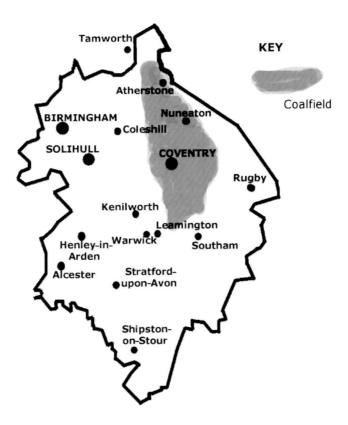

Fig 47. Warwickshire coalfield

More attention was directed to education at this time and a number of schools were established in the county including Coventry Grammar School in 1545, King Edward's School in Birmingham in 1552, Solihull School in 1560 and Rugby School in 1567. They were usually built on the edge of town on open country or existing parkland.

Some towns gradually became known as the centre for particular trades. Stratford was recognised for making gloves, Arden was an area known for retting or softening flax and hemp and Birmingham became a centre for a great number of trades including metal working of many kinds as well as tanning, hemp & flax retting, brick and tile manufacture and pottery. In Alcester there were many butchers and tanners at this time and two flour mills were built in Kineton in 1565. There was a coal mine at Parkview in the parish of Bedworth in 1572 and the Bedworth area was well known for coal mining from 1595. From 1598 there was also growth of coal mining at Foleshill and Coventry. The extent of the coalfield is shown in Fig 47. The mill pool at Chesterton was mentioned in 1554.

Roads, Country Houses, The First 'Green Belt', Kenilworth Castle, Churches and Manor Houses, Monasteries

In the sixteenth century there was a major landmark in progress as parishes were made responsible for the maintenance of roads by an Act of Parliament in 1555. The Act also required that every person must provide the equivalent of three days free labour each year to maintain and improve the roads. However the law did not have an immediate effect and there was little significant improvement of the roads achieved for around another hundred years.

Alveston Manor, Alveston	Moat House, Coundon
Arbury Hall, Arbury	Moat House, Keresley
Arlescote House, Warmington	Moor Hall, Sutton Coldfield
Barrells Hall, Ullenhall	New House, Coventry
Berry Hall, Solihull	Newbold Comyn, Leamington
Bishops Itchington House, Bishops Itchington	Offchurch Bury, Offchurch
Cawston House, Dunchurch	Packington Hall, Great Packington
Compton Wynyates, Compton Wynyates	Packwood House, Lapworth
Emscote Hall, Emscote	Pipes Mill, Stoneleigh
Fetherstone House, Tanworth	Pool Hall, Sutton Coldfield
Fletchamstead Hall, Coventry	Pooley Hall, Polesworth
Goldicote House, Alderminster	Radford Hall, Radford Semele
Grange The, Church Lawford	Sheldon Hall, Sheldon
Haseley Old Manor, Haseley	Shuckburgh Hall, Shuckburgh
Hole House, Wootton Wawen	Skilts, Studley
Hungerley Hall, Wyken	Ungley House, Wyken
Kingshurst Hall, Coleshill	Weddington Hall, Weddington
Knowle Hall Old, Knowle	Weston-under-Wetherley Hall, Weston-under-Wetherley
Ladbroke Hall, Ladbroke	Wharley Hall, Barston
Libbards House, Solihull	Whitley Abbey, Coventry
Longbridge House, Warwick	Windmill House, Rowington
Milcote House, Weston on Avon	Wormleighton Manor, Wormleighton

Fig 48. Some houses built in the sixteenth century

Fig 49. The large church at Brailes, known as the 'Cathedral of the Feldon'

This was the busiest century so far for building large country houses, indicative of the growth in wealth, and with their grounds taking up significant areas in the countryside. Great houses were built at Coughton Court, Packwood and Charlecote. Coventry Castle still existed in the sixteenth century.

On the national stage in 1580 one of the first ever conservation measures in England was the creation of a form of 'green belt' when Queen Elizabeth I issued an edict that there should not be any new building within three miles of any of the gates of London.

Wood and timber continued to be important sources of materials for a number of uses. Hedges themselves were a useful source of wood and it is said that the heyday of hedgerow trees was from 1500 to 1750. An extensive survey of trees in Tanworth-in-Arden was carried out around 1500. One example of uses is that oak bark was valuable in the tanning of leather. Medieval woodland usually had a substantial boundary denoted by a bank and external ditch and remnants of these can be found today. From 1540 to 1543 there was a mini ice age and the prices of timber rose by 75%.

In this period timber framed buildings often had close-studded walls because timber remained plentiful. In the following centuries there were wider spaces between the timbers which were filled with wattle and daub and the timbers were of lighter section. There was a high volume of building in Tudor times and a considerable fragment of it still survives. For example Charlecote house was built in 1558 in the Tudor style, although it was much altered in the nineteenth century. The Tudor building revolution caused most existing buildings to be rebuilt or significantly altered. There is little remaining from earlier times. Arden in particular has many surviving brick and timber farmhouses from the Tudor period. Preston Bagot Manor was built in 1550 and Haselor Manor Farm dates from this time and it has tall and ornate chimneys which were a status symbol in the Elizabethan period. Church Farm at Morton Bagot was built in 1580 with close studding in the lower storey which was more in the style of the south of the county.

Unfortunately no Tudor buildings survive in Nuneaton but it is recorded that stalls in the Market Place of the town moved into permanent buildings in Tudor times. The original street plan from 1540 still remains in Nuneaton but in 1543 the town had no more than 180 houses. In contrast at the other end of the spectrum of events the castle at Henley-in-Arden was demolished and the village was in serious decline.

Kenilworth Castle was probably at its peak of development around 1575 and the large water feature known as The Pleasaunce dates from this time. Conspicuous remnants of the earthworks which contained the lakes can still be seen from public footpaths to the west of the castle.

The main earlier buildings which survive from this period are churches, manor houses and some vernacular buildings. One surviving timber framed church is within the later stone structure at Morton Bagot. The Reformation led to the demolition of many great abbeys and priories. For example most of Stoneleigh Abbey was demolished leaving only the gatehouse. There was a chapel at Attleborough in Nuneaton from 1563 but in parallel with the rest of the county Nuneaton Priory was dissolved in 1539. There was also an abbey at Alcester but it closed in 1536.

Coventry had at least four monasteries at the beginning of the century. There was a Benedictine Priory, the Franciscans at Greyfriars, the Carmelites at Whitefriars and the Carthusians at Charterhouse. The dissolution of the monasteries in 1536 wrecked trade and the population of the city fell by about two-thirds from 10,000 to 3,000. After the reformation the monasteries no longer provided care for the poor and sick and almshouses began to be built for this purpose. A major landmark in Coventry was the 57 feet high Coventry Cross in Cross Cheaping. It was completed in 1543 but taken down in 1771.

SIXTEENTH CENTURY

In this century Coventry lost the villages of Asthill and Horwell which were abandoned and the rural county lost Chesterton and Wormleighton villages. During this period many villagers continued to live in huts of straw and mud of which nothing now remains.

Chapter Eleven

Seventeenth Century

**Enclosure Continues, Hedgerows, Rugby Cattle Market,
Turnips and Clover Introduced.**

The enclosure of the open fields continued in a piecemeal way,parish by parish, and in this century this was recognised in each case by a Local Inclosure Act. An integral part of the enclosures and the consequent dividing up of the land was the planting of hedges. The species of plants in the hedges today depends on the people who did the planting and what was available and also what has self-seeded over the years. An older hedge generally has more species and some research suggests that each species indicates a period of as little as 30 years in the life of the hedge. The presence of spindle and wayfaring trees suggests that a hedge is old whereas hawthorn, blackthorn and elder are often more recent planting. Various species self-seed into hedges but farmers are always quick to grub out any seedlings of yew because they are poisonous to livestock. Hedges are very valuable for man as a kind of linear coppice and they were regarded as a valuable asset for providing wood. The line of the hedges planted as boundaries to enclosure fields are arbitrary and tend not to follow the contours of the land.

Sometimes when fields were enclosed it was agreed that paths, roads and even streams should be diverted. Especially in the later parliamentary enclosures the fields were often large and rectangular and new wide, straight roads were marked out on the documents. Enclosure agreements were usually modified to leave some allotments and pastures as well as enclosed fields. A lot of the open fields agricultural system remained in Warwickshire in this century and many areas were not enclosed until the final parliamentary enclosures in the nineteenth century. A substantial area of common land was ploughed up following the enclosures.

In the Nuneaton area, Attleborough originally had three large open fields. In this century Ashow was enclosed in 1649, Wolston in 1692 and Leamington Priors in 1698 and other villages enclosed were Bramcote, Barnacle, Copston Parva and Shelford. After enclosure the many fields which were created at Chesterton were given such names as Pleck, Plum Pudding, Seven Acres, Thompsons Ground, Warrens Meadow, Brick Kiln, Marl Pit Ground, Stytch (Norse for furthest), Flax Ground, Hemp Meadow, Wodground (Woad), Town

Close, Shoulder of Mutton, Thistley Ground, Mill Hill, Barn Hill, Sallibed (Willow).

In order to service the new farming enterprises the Rugby cattle market was established in the seventeenth century. It had been traditional to slaughter many cattle on Michaelmas Day, 29 September, because there was insufficient material to feed the animals during the winter. However, in the seventeenth century there was sufficient feed, at least in the Coleshill area, to keep cattle through the colder months. Turnips were introduced as a field crop around 1645. The importation of cattle, sheep, and swine was forbidden in 1664 and from 1688 there was a bounty of 5s. per quarter on the export of wheat and there was a high duty on imports. It is perhaps surprising to learn that the first manufactured fertilizers were made as early as the early seventeenth century.

Fig 50. Hunningham, an impeccably restored cottage

Growth of Manufacture, The Brick Industry, Turnpikes, River Avon

In this century wealth generally increased and various kinds of manufactured goods became more widely affordable for ordinary people. Blacksmiths were frequently found in villages and they were able to manufacture a surprising range of items. Textile manufacture and glass making also had a big impact on the Midlands in the seventeenth century. From the latter part of the seventeenth century deforestation was drastic which meant that there was less wood for burning and consequently there was rapid growth in coal mining. In 1612 the 'Great Mine' at Bedworth employed 500 people and from 1687 to 1730 coal was plentiful in the area. In 1618 the mine at Bedworth was abandoned because of flooding but it reopened in the following year. However from the 1690s the Coventry mines were closing because of flooding.

Fig 51. Baginton Oak

Cap and hat making was a significant business in a number of places including Coventry, Atherstone, Nuneaton and Rugby. In Bedworth in 1690 the weaving trade grew rapidly as Protestants belonging to a group known as Huguenots fled from France. Coventry became especially known in this period for watch-making. The town of Coleshill had very few shops which we would recognise today and people traded from backyard workshops. Alcester became known for leather as a satellite of the major centre at Worcester. Although it has been claimed that needle making started in the Alcester area in Norman times it is likely that it was thriving in this century. The industry began in probably in

Studley and from 1670 needles were being made in factories in the town of Alcester.

As building boomed clay pits continued to be developed and brick production increased. Alcester boasted four or five brickworks at this time. A stone quarry at Attleborough near Nuneaton was already well established.

The notable windmill at Chesterton was built in 1632 and the watermill in 1634. There was another windmill south-east of the green but no trace remains.

In the seventeenth century various groups of landowners decided to take responsibility for the maintenance of roads and established turnpike trusts which raised money from tolls. The very first order under the Turnpike Act 1663 in England applied to a stretch of the Great North Road in Hertfordshire. This process developed from 1663 to 1836. However the first turnpike in Warwickshire was not authorized until 1724. At the end of the seventeenth century parish rates were raised to repair roads. The three main roads through Warwickshire in this century were the road from London to Coventry and Shrewsbury, the road from Gloucester to Stratford and the road from Oxford to Coventry. We have seen that enclosure often led to new or rerouted local roads.

From the mid seventeenth century until the nineteenth century the droving of sheep and cattle from the countryside to cities remained common. There are roads named Welsh Road East and West at Southam, probably used for this purpose. During a similar period of time improvements to navigation on rivers meant big changes for transport and with the upgrading of the navigation of the River Avon Stratford-upon-Avon became a staging post for products from Bristol into the Birmingham area.

Large Houses, Public Houses,
Civil War.

This was another busy century for the building of all types and at least 55 large houses were built in Warwickshire (see Fig 53). As suitable timber became more and more scarce timber-framed houses were built with wider spaces between the timbers so that less wood was used. This evolution in construction methods can be used to date some of the remaining houses. There was plenty of clay for bricks being dug out and baked from the middle of the seventeenth century and therefore more brick houses were built.

Packwood House was started in 1650 and is noted for the topiary trees which are said to represent the Sermon on the Mount. There is a cruck house at Walcote which probably dates from this time. The history of public houses is a study of its own but they were uncommon before this date and many of them were built or converted from existing buildings in this century mainly as inns for pilgrims. The Royal Oak at Whatcote was a very early inn.

Fig 52. Charlecote House. A much modified and restored Elizabethan house.

The unusual lychgate at Long Compton was possibly built as a priest's house. The Manor house on Image Hill at Chesterton was rebuilt with a classical façade in 1632.

Many racecourses were constructed in Britain during the seventeenth and eighteenth centuries. Racing in Warwick took place as early as 1694 when it was introduced in the hope of attracting wealthy investors to the town to help rebuild it after the fire. It is believed that the present location of the racecourse was first used in about 1728. Stratford upon Avon racecourse is rather later and dates from about 1755. Alcester and Stratford-upon-Avon became major centres for the sale and barter of goods with shops and markets and they are now known as 'market towns'. Dunchurch also became a thriving market town in the seventeenth and eighteenth centuries.

Ragley Hall near Alcester was built in 1678 but the impressive portico was not added until a century later in 1780. Coombe Abbey was built in the 1680s. Charlecote House garden was laid out about 1696 and the Charlecote deer park was developed somewhat later by Capability Brown in the 1750s. On the other hand in this century Brandon Castle and Mount Grevill at Milcote were

Admington Hall, Admington	Holyfast Grange, Aston
Alder Mill, Atherstone	Honiley Hall, Honiley
Allesley Park, Allesley	Honington Hall, Honington
Alscot Park, Atherstone-on-Stour	Jerrings Hall, Tanworth
Alveston House, Alveston	Libbards House, Sutton Coldfield
Ansley Hall, Ansley	Little Compton Manor, Little
Ansty Hall, Ansty	Compton
Aston Hall, Aston	Merevale Hall, Atherstone
Atherstone Hall, Atherstone	Moat House, Sheldon
Barton Manor, Barton-on-the-Heath	Moxhull Hall, Wishaw
Berkswell Hall, Berkswell	Newbold Pacey Hall, Newbold
Billesley Manor/Hall, Billesley	Pacey
Bilton Hall, Dunchurch	Newnham Paddox, Monks Kirby
Birdingbury Hall, Birdingbury	Penns Hall, Sutton Coldfield
Blyth Hall, Shustoke	Peter Hall, Combe Fields
Broom Court, Bidford	Radway Grange, Radway
Chadshunt House, Chadshunt	Ragley Hall, Alcester
Chesterton House, Chesterton	Snitterfield House, Snitterfield
Claverdon House, Claverdon	St John's House, Warwick
Clifford Chambers House, Clifford	Umberslade Hall, Tanworth-in-
Chambers	Arden
Clopton House, Stratford	Upton House, Edge Hill
Erdington Hall, Erdington	Walton Hall, Walton
Farnborough Hall, Farnborough	Warwick Priory, Warwick
Frog Hall, Wolston	Watergall House, Watergall
Grendon Hall, Grendon	Welcombe House, Stratford
Hall End Hall, Polesworth	Wellesbourne Hall, Wellesbourne
Hoare Hall, Over Whitacre	Weston in Arden Hall, Bulkington
Holmes House, Bishops Itchington	Woodcote, Leek Wootton
	Wootton Hall, Wootton Wawen
	Wroxall Abbey, Wroxall

Fig 53. List of Houses Built in the Seventeenth Century

demolished. The Great Fire in Warwick occurred in 1694 which destroyed many timber-framed buildings and a lot of stone and bricks were needed to rebuild

97

the town. Preston-on-Stour was largely built in this century and is today perhaps the most unspoilt village remaining in Warwickshire.

Villages which were deserted in this century include Upper and Lower Radbourne, Compton Wynyates, Wormleighton, Little Dassett, Hodwell, Stoneton and Smercote Magna near Bedworth.

A major disruption of life in England was the Civil War which lasted from 1638 to 1651 and many castles were damaged in the hostilities. Whereas Warwick Castle withstood a 14 day siege from the Royalists, nearby Kenilworth Castle was seriously damaged by Cromwell. The Battle of Edgehill took place on 23rd October 1642 near Kineton and the church walls in Chadshunt show damage from gunfire during the War. There is a monument commemorating the battle on Banbury Road, Kineton. Parliamentary troops burned Wormleighton in 1642 and the village has never recovered. There was significant emigration and loss of population following the Civil War. In consequence in 1650 the population of Britain was somewhere between five and six million. The population of Warwickshire towns is quite well established since registration began and in Coventry in 1680 there were between 5,000 and 10,000 people and the size of Birmingham was similar. The population of Bedworth 1665 was 823 and that of Chilvers Coton was 850 in 1674 while the population of Attleborough in 1660 was 320.

In the seventeenth and eighteenth centuries the social structure evolved to a complex hierarchy ranging from dukes, earls, and baronets at the top, through gentlemen and squires, vicars and rectors next, then yeomen, husbandmen, farmers and parish officials, then labourers and craftsmen and finally cottagers and servants.

A strange tale about Coventry is recorded that Mother Shipton forecast in the fifteenth century that the walls would be felled by a pigeon. In reality they were destroyed by the mayor, Thomas Pidgeon, in 1662 but some gates did survive.

On a different theme a chalybeate spring at Ilmington was famous for its healing qualities for a while from 1684.

Chapter Twelve

Eighteenth Century

Fig 54. Chesterton windmill. A graceful
stone structure designed by Inigo Jones

The Enclosures Movement Gathers Pace

Over much of the county the farmland had remained similar in appearance
for many centuries, apart from the few areas which had been enclosed in the
seventeenth century or converted for use as parkland or forest. Enclosure
gathered pace particularly in the second half of the eighteenth century changing
the appearance of much of the landscape for ever. The period from 1720 to 1840
is known as the time of 'The Great Enclosures'. Around 1760 was also the time
when the great industrial and agrarian revolution began.

Unlike the earlier enclosures the new grids of fields usually largely ignored the old pattern of the shapes of the fields. Enclosure at this time was carried out by parliament granting a local Inclosure Act and over 5200 of these acts were passed by Parliament for the whole of England and Wales. Note that we refer to Enclosures but at this time the legal spelling was Inclosure. It is important to be aware that the administrative processes for enclosure which were used at this time required the consent of 75% of the tenants and landowners. It is likely that those in power used various forms of persuasion.

1700-1710	1
1710-1720	8
1720-1730	33
1730-1740	35
1740-1750	38
1750-1760	156
1760-1770	424
1770-1780	642
1780-1790	287
1790-1800	506
1800-1810	906

Fig 55. Numbers of Enclosure Acts in England and Wales

There was a total of about 175 Enclosure Acts applying to Warwickshire. The first was in Lighthorne in 1720 and the last was in Langley in 1835. For example about 3300 acres were enclosed in Priors Marston in 1758, 2000 acres at Southam in 1761, 2000 acres in Napton in 1778 and 3600 acres in Brailes in 1787. Kinwarton had six open fields in the eighteenth century until enclosure in 1803. In Alcester the mid-eighteenth century land tenure was very confused because it was largely held by the six medium to large farms in the parish named Alcester Heath Farm, Alcester Lodge Farm, Alcester Warren Farm, Kings Coughton House, Beauchamp Court and Moat House Farm. Enclosure in 1771 dealt with 617 acres which was only one third of the parish and no new farms were created after enclosure.

The primary advantage of enclosures was that farmers had control of whole fields and could take decisions without having to obtain the agreement of the whole number of other people who used the field. They also facilitated the use of commons and wastelands for productive purposes. The land could therefore be used more efficiently and fewer people were required to work the land. As a consequence many people lost their livelihood and had to move to towns where they turned their hands to commerce by making things or running shops. The real impact of the enclosures was that it changed the physical and social structure of the country. Some of the consequences of enclosure were that it facilitated the rearing of livestock, farming was banished from parkland and there were tree planting campaigns to counteract the felling which took place. Roads were also often rationalized and new farms were soon built among the fields away from the existing villages. Fodder crops such as clover and sainfoin were sown from the middle of the eighteenth century.

Some more of the enclosures in the eighteenth century included Bubbenhall (Bubnel)(1726), Little Kineton (1733), Hillmorton (1754), Radway (1756), Priors Marston (1758), Southam (1761), Preston-on-Stour (1762 to 1766) and Grandborough (1766). Also enclosed in the early part of the century were Bulkington, Burton Hastings, Shilton and Wolvey. Under the provisions of the Inclosure Act 1767 the land from Whitnash to Radford Semele was enclosed and there were later enclosures at Bedworth (1770), Warwick St Nicholas (1773), Avon Dassett (1780), Weston-under-Wetherley (1780), Kineton (1792) and Austrey (1793). Other enclosures towards the end of the century were Pailton, Stretton-under-Fosse and Harborough Magna. Kineton had a number of common fields but after enclosure the field names of Park Piece, Flaxlands, Shortacres and Glosters Green were lost. The open fields at Coleshill had a four crop rotation but 900 acres of them were enclosed in 1780 with new fields ranging in size from 2 to 30 acres. Lord (Turnip) Townshend is credited with the introduction of a four crop rotation in 1730 made up of clover, roots and two cereals in the cycle.

One unfortunate consequence of the enclosures was that the red horse cut into the hillside in the Vale of the Red Horse near Tysoe was destroyed when the land was enclosed in 1798. It had been a tradition to clean up the large figure of a horse on Palm Sunday each year.

Hedgerows

It should be remembered that although there were generally large fields there were many hedgerows before enclosure. Hedges had been used for many centuries as boundaries to mark property and to keep animals in the places where they were wanted. Some estimates are that as many as 50% of hedges date from some time during the period from the Bronze Age to the end of the seventeenth century. Plants were dug from woods and existing hedges to put in the new hedges and there was a nursery trade in young trees and saplings from the fourteenth century. Trees are obviously very important in the landscape and 1750 was probably the year that saw the peak number of hedgerow trees being planted. These were primarily oak, ash and elm. There was a marked decline in the planting of hedges from 1750 because of enclosures and subsidies. At that time it is likely that the total length of hedges was at least equal to those that exist now.

Model Farms, Advances in Scientific Farming

The concept of model farms was introduced from the middle of this century. Some forward-thinking landlords saw that better use could be made of the land and a four crop rotation was developed, land was drained and efficient designs for farm buildings were built which became known as 'model' farms. Some model farms were designed by the leading designers and architects of the day. There were model farms at Harbury, Southam and on the Studley Castle estate.

Fig 56. The Great West Wing of Stoneleigh Abbey,

There were many other notable events related to agriculture in this century. Heaths declined from 1700 and there was an inquiry into an acute shortage of timber in 1791. Grass and clover seeds were available on sale from about 1700 and with the concentration on rearing sheep for wool from 1789 England became a corn-importing country. Swedes were first grown in 1795. There was much concern about an outbreak of sheep-rot in 1739. The elm tree was very common and some place names such as Whichford remember the alternative name of wice or witch elm.

This was a century of innovation in farming. In 1733 Jethro Tull published his book entitled 'Horse-hoeing Husbandry' which exhorted farmers to plough in rows and to hoe between them. This was a major advance in scientific farming. In 1760 the innovative farmer, Robert Bakewell, took control of the family farm near Loughborough and began experimenting. Bakewell pioneered grassland irrigation, diverting rivers and building canals to flood the fields. He also established experimental plots to test different manures and flooding methods. He later strengthened the bloodlines of cattle, sheep and pigs by his advances in stock breeding. He controlled the mating of animals instead of allowing males and females to graze together all the time and he also kept rams for neighbouring farmers to use for breeding. These ideas revolutionised the general approach to farming. We now see individual fields of very similar cattle or sheep whereas before Bakewell's time the appearance of the animals in a single field would be very varied. Bakewell bred animals for the tastes of his time and his breeds were generally very fatty. Tastes have changed and his breeds are no longer popular but his breeding methods still continue. In 1764 another innovator, Joseph Elkington, introduced a new drainage system. His local claim to fame is that he was baptised in Stretton-on-Dunsmore in 1740.

More Country Houses

Bordesley Hall, Birmingham	Little Kineton House, Little Kineton
Bourton Hall, Bourton-on-Dunsmore	Malvern Hall, Solihull
Bramcote Hall, Polesworth	Meriden Hall, Meriden
Compton Verney, Kineton	Moor Hall, Sutton Coldfield
Coton House, Churchover	Newbold Revel/St Pauls, Stretton-under-Fosse
Eathorpe Hall, Eathorpe	
Edgbaston Hall, Edgbaston	Oldbury Hall, Oldbury
Elmdon Hall, Elmdon	Radbrook Manor, Preston-on-Stour
Four Oaks Hall, Sutton Coldfield	Sherbourne Park, Sherbourne
Foxcote, Ilmington	Springfield House, Temple Balsall
Hams Hall, Lea Marston	Stivichall Hall, Coventry
Hurley Hall, Hurley	Westham House, Barford
Idlicote House, Idlicote	Windmill House, Dunchurch

Fig 57. Country houses built in the eighteenth century

Also during the century a number of houses were rebuilt by wealthy landowners who wished to keep up with contemporary fashion and had the funds to do it. These included Elmdon Hall, Packington Hall, Compton Verney, Newbold Revel and Bilton Hall. Arbury Hall was rebuilt in this century and is a gem of Gothic revival architecture.

Coleshill had developed well in this century and in 1725 Daniel Defoe described it as *"a small but very handsome market town"*. A notable school built at this time was the Birmingham Blue Coat School in 1724. Great Packington church, built in 1790, may lay claim to be the finest eighteenth century church in the county. This church has a square plan with four corner turrets and is in the neo-classical style in red brick and is topped with domes and finials. Daily justice was administered locally and Church Farm near the Manor in Morton Bagot has a barn which was called the Court House in 1744.

Fig 58. Berkswell, this original village pump was restored in 2000

104

Industrial Revolution, Coal Mining, Windmills

The Industrial Revolution began to gather momentum in this century and more and more factories were built across the countryside. However Warwickshire just missed out on a landmark event because it was intended to erect the first Newcomen steam engine at Griff near Nuneaton in 1711. However the first one was actually built at Dudley and the engine at Griff was not completed until 1714. Mining around Bedworth continued with this ground-breaking atmospheric engine being erected for pumping water from a mine. From 1727 collieries at Bedworth, Hawkesbury and Wykin were at their peak. There were as many as fifty collieries in this small area by 1725. However discontent over rates of pay led to sabotage of some mines in Bedworth in 1728 and 1729. Unfortunately mines soon became worked out and some were closing from as early as 1765.

Windmills also developed further at this time and many of these mills became conspicuous features in the landscape. In Kineton the Pittern Hill stone windmill tower was built around 1725. Water wheels also continued to be widely used to drive machinery and were important for the milling of flour, fulling of cloth and in the production of paper and cotton and many of the associated buildings are still standing.

There was growth in the number of military establishments in this century with the construction of shooting ranges, training schools and barracks. For example, in Coventry in 1793, the Black Bull and surrounding grounds were converted to barracks for use during the war with France and the area is now the landmark Barracks car park in the city centre.

The economy was changing quickly. Home-grown trees were reduced in economic importance because their traditional uses were being replaced as there were new building materials and coal for energy. However there was even a market for imported timber alongside many other imported goods.

Canals and Turnpikes

In the annals of the transport history of Britain, and Warwickshire, the eighteenth century was the century of the canal. In order to construct a canal it was first necessary to acquire an Act of Parliament and canals were designed, approved and built in the north and the south of the country. Unfortunately the various canals were built for different sizes of boats. The first Act for Warwickshire was obtained in 1751 to make the River Avon navigable and this was eventually made possible from Tewkesbury to just upstream of Stratford-upon-Avon at Alveston. The Oxford Canal was built to provide access to the River Thames; it was authorised by Acts from 1769 and opened between 1774 and 1790. The Coventry Canal was authorised in 1768 to provide a link through Bedworth to the Trent and Mersey Canal and was fully open by 1789. In the north the Birmingham and Fazeley Canal was authorised in 1783 and opened in 1789. In 1793 and 1794 the Birmingham and Warwick and the Warwick and Braunston Canals were authorized. The latter eventually terminated at Napton with a junction with the Oxford Canal and they both opened in 1799. The Stratford canal was also authorized in 1793 but was much delayed and did not reach Stratford until 1816. Notable features of this canal are the iron trough aqueducts at Edstone (Bearley), Wootton Wawen and Yarningale Common. Edstone is the longest iron aqueduct in England. There was soon a rough cross of canals joining together the rivers Trent, Mersey, Severn and Thames. At their height there were 3700 miles of canals in Britain but now only about 2000 miles are still navigable. Many became derelict and unnavigable in the twentieth century. One of the first to be restored was the Stratford-upon-Avon Canal.

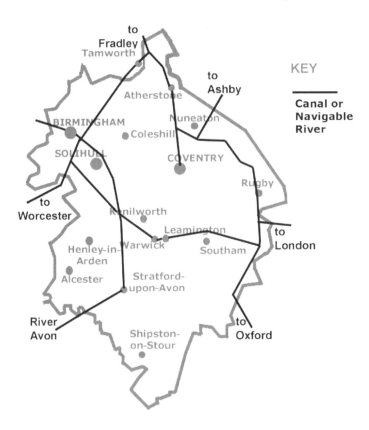

Fig 59. Canals and navigable rivers of Warwickshire

Some canals took very circuitous routes as they followed the contours of the land to avoid building locks and earthworks and later on embankments and cuttings were sometimes built to shorten routes and reduce delays at locks. One stretch near Smethwick has at various times been at three different levels and it is now in a deep cutting. Parts of the Oxford Canal were very devious and a section remains near Fenny Compton where it is necessary to travel nearly five miles to achieve just over one mile as the crow flies. Other bends were later replaced with a more direct route on an embankment or in a cutting. For example a long disused loop remains near Newbold-on-Avon and the mouth of a tunnel which was abandoned is visible in Newbold-on-Avon churchyard. British Waterways is now the custodian of most of the canals and is thus responsible for 2000 listed structures and 64 sites of special scientific interest throughout Britain. Canals have left a significant impact on the landscape with flights of locks, embankments, cuttings, aqueducts, reservoirs, lock cottages and bridges being the most obvious features.

Fig 60. A lock cottage at Lowsonford on the Stratford Canal.
The design of the roof is attributed to the skills of bridge-builders

Notable canal lock flights in Warwickshire are at Hatton, Lapworth, Hillmorton, Atherstone and Napton. Novel bridges across the canal are found on the Stratford-upon-Avon canal where the bridge is so narrow that there is no room for a towpath and therefore there is a gap down the middle of the bridge for the towline. The canals of the Midlands were built to take boats seven feet wide and seventy feet long. The boats usually travelled in pairs and a pair could carry up to sixty tons of cargo. Initially the boats, sometimes called barges but more properly called narrow boats, were hauled by horses. Canals have now become widely used today for recreation - for boating, fishing, cycling and walking.

Fig 61. The Oxford Canal at Napton.
A classic view from Windmill Hill which is frequently seen in calendars

Many roads were in a very poor condition at this time but this was to improve as turnpikes were being established in a many places. Turnpikes were named after the gate across the road which was used to stop travellers at the toll house. The first Turnpike Act in Britain was passed in 1663 and was followed by many more. The first turnpike road in Warwickshire was the road from Old Stratford in Northamptonshire to Dunchurch in 1707. This was followed by the road from Dunchurch to Stonebridge (Meriden Hill) in 1724 and the road from Birmingham to Edge Hill via Stratford in 1725. The Droitwich to Stratford turnpike passed through Alcester in 1754.

In 1725 the roads around Bedworth were reported to be in a very poor state. The Coventry to Bedworth turnpike was established in 1755 and in 1760 the turnpike from Stonebridge to Chester through Coleshill was set up. In 1761

Watling Street became a turnpike which presented a new route for long distance travel and was a challenge to the previously busy road through Coleshill and the coaching inns in the town. The first turnpike in the Kineton area was from Wellesbourne to Upton on Edge Hill in 1770 and the Evesham Bridge to Alcester turnpike was established in 1778. There were at least 24 turnpikes in the county by the end of the eighteenth century and a total of 42 by 1852. Another Act in 1773 made it easier to re-route roads. Harwoods House at Chesterton was a staging post on the turnpike from Warwick to Banbury. Toll Houses survive at Clopton Bridge in Stratford-upon-Avon, Newbold-on-Stour, Weethley Gate near Dunnington and at Arrow. A good example of a toll house from Little Malvern in Worcestershire is preserved at the Avoncroft museum near Bromsgrove.

Fig 62. Some of the turnpikes in Warwickshire

The technology of road construction owes its progress to three key men of this period, John Metcalfe, Thomas Telford and John Loudon McAdam. They all realised that effective drainage was essential to ensure a long life for a road. A number of minor roads have gradually been lost since the enclosures and in the 1930s it was decided not to continue to tar many of them. A neglected road can be lost to the growth of blackthorn in as little as ten years and a road running along a hillside can easily be lost completely as the hill erodes unless it is frequently used and properly maintained.

Population Growth, Birth of Conservation, Country House Gardens

The population of Britain as a whole increased in this century. The population of Warwickshire increased from 96,000 in 1701 to 140,000 in 1750 and then to around 200,000 in 1801. This definition of Warwickshire included Birmingham, Coventry and Solihull. Within Warwickshire the population of Kineton in 1774 was between 600 and 650 and this had increased to 750 by 1801. Elsewhere the population of Bedworth had reached 1220 by 1730. Early in the eighteenth century only about 50% of the population was working in agriculture.

In the late eighteenth century there was a growth of interest among the upper classes in Britain in nature and a romantic view of the countryside developed which was far removed from the reality and drudgery of working the land. A word that was frequently used to describe the 'best' scenery was 'sublime' and the Romantic movement found rugged and remote areas appealing. William Wordsworth is seen by many as the founder of conservation and his interest was derived from his affection for his beloved Lake District. It became fashionable to acquire pictures of landscapes but, on the contrary, the Scottish poet, James Thomson (1700 to 1748) wrote –

"But who can paint like Nature? Can imagination boast, amid its gay creation, hues like hers?"

Fashion also dictated that those who could afford it should create country houses with formal gardens in an attempt to manufacture a vision of sublime Arcadia at home. Many of the designs for gardens of these houses were based on the paintings of Claude (Claude Gelee known as Claude Lorrain), Nicolas Poussin and Salvator Rosa. There are particularly fine eighteenth gardens at Compton Wynyates, Newnham Paddox, Four Oaks Hall and Weston Hall. From

110

the 1730s parks were made more naturalistic but often with follies to provide focal points.

The famous garden landscapers William Kent, Lancelot (Capability) Brown, Humphry Repton and Charles Bridgeman were very busily occupied at this time. In Warwickshire, Capability Brown reshaped several gardens and parks including Warwick Castle, Compton Wynyates, Compton Verney, Snitterfield House, Newnham Paddox, Packington Hall, Edgbaston Hall and Charlecote House. Brown referred to himself as a 'place maker' although the present-day term of 'landscape architect' had already been coined. Humphry Repton designed the landscaping of the grounds of Stoneleigh Abbey and Moseley Hall. These were all examples of landscape in the 'Grand Manner' and John Milton's 'Paradise Lost' describes a lost landscape the like of which was never to be seen again except in landscaped parks such as these.

Nucleation of Settlements, Fox Hunting

The trend for people to move from small settlements and hamlets to larger villages, a process called nucleation, continued and to a large extent those villages tended to be designed and planned by the local landowners. Rows of matching cottages which were built at this time can still be found in villages in the county. There were fewer small farmers than in the past and there was a growing trend for large landowners to employ workers directly.

Fox hunting also became fashionable and led to the building of stables and kennels and to continue the interest in equestrianism the racecourse was constructed at Warwick in 1728.

The church remained important in society and the vicar was usually central to village life in the late eighteenth century. The rectory or vicarage was often a large and imposing building and many of these remain today.

Deserted Villages, Village Growth

For various reasons some more villages became deserted. For example Hunscote had disappeared by the end of the eighteenth century as it was enclosed within the landscaped park of Charlecote House. Other villages such as Southam were in decline by 1750 but were far from deserted.

On the other hand some other villages became more important during this century. 40% of the villagers of Henley-in-Arden in 1710 had a craft or trade and there was a big revival of the town in the period 1770 to 1840, in the coaching era, as roads improved. In Wolfhamcote and Grandborough in 1760 50% of residents had a trade and the situation was similar in Tysoe by 1790. In 1720 Solihull, Birmingham, Nuneaton, Atherstone and Coventry were thriving. The unique development of the hamlet of Leamington Priors into the Royal town of Leamington Spa as a pleasure resort is remarkable. In 1783 there was only a church, a well, a mill, two inns, stocks and a pound for strays. The building of baths and successful marketing of the springs in the town in the next few years changed the hamlet into a busy town.

Estate villages were a feature of the eighteenth and nineteenth centuries. Landowners demolished whole villages and rebuilt them a convenient distance away from their country houses. The new village was often smaller than before and some residents had to move away. These new villages were usually provided with a school, village hall or reading room although inns were rare. Most of the residents worked for the landowner.

Chapter Thirteen

Nineteenth Century

Introduction, The Final Enclosures,
Mechanisation

This was a century of almost incredible changes in many aspects of life and this chapter is therefore one of the longest in this book. There is almost nothing that did not change. Industrialisation attracted people away from the land and led to the spread of town boundaries into the countryside on a scale not seen before. Also the mechanisation of agriculture increased in leaps and bounds and this soon changed the look of the land. The final stages of enclosure also took place in the early years of the century.

The enclosure of the open fields continued in Warwickshire until about 1867. For example in Long Compton 2,238 acres of land was enclosed in 1812 and as much as 495 acres of the land was retained for common use. Before enclosure Long Compton had 4 open fields named Yeardley, Colloway, March and Bartongrove. The enclosure document for the village stated that 4 foot wide ditches were to be dug around the new fields with a fence on either side of a hawthorn hedge. Unfortunately the hedges planted following these later enclosures often included very few trees or even none at all.

John Clare (1793 to 1864), the Peasant Poet, was extremely upset at the effect of enclosure on the countryside that he knew and loved. He wrote about his sorrow at the tidying up of the countryside consequent on the enclosures. He considered that enclosure forbade access to the land, it caused trees to be felled and brooks to dry up, it made peasants into slaves, it created little fields and caused houses to be pulled down. He wrote two elegies to England before the enclosures called 'Remembrances' and 'To A Fallen Elm'. He urged people not to forsake the valleys by pursuing progress. Here is one verse from 'Remembrances'.

By Langley bush I roam but the bush hath left its hill
On cowper green I stray tis a desert strange and chill
And spreading lea close oak ere decay had penned its will
To the axe of the spoiler and self interest fell a prey
And cross berry way and old round oaks narrow lane

With its hollow trees like pulpits I shall never see again
Inclosure like a Buonaparte let not a thing remain
It levelled every bush and tree and levelled every hill
And hung the moles for traitors - though the brook is running still
It runs a naked brook cold and chill.

George Eliot (1819 to 1880), the author, who lived at Griff House in the Nuneaton area for some time, wrote lovingly about the countryside and must have been inspired by the Warwickshire countryside. She wrote about the plight of the poor and the divisions in society. In The Mill on the Floss she wrote

"How lovely the little river is, with its dark changing wavelets! It seems to me like a living companion while I wander along the bank, and listen to its low, placid voice . . ."

L T C (Tom) Rolt (1910 to 1974) wrote that

"...the enclosures paved the way for an era of 'high farming' with improved stock breeding and methods of cultivation. But the misery and abject poverty which this ruthless dispossession caused among the erstwhile commoners of England ultimately led to a cheap food policy which was to bring about the ruin of English agriculture..."

The process of enclosure was simplified by the Inclosure Consolidation Act of 1801 and later the local enclosure Acts operated together with the provisions of the General Inclosure Act 1836. After 1845 there were few local acts and most enclosures were under the General Inclosure Act 1845. These late enclosures meant that large areas of commons, former royal forests and grazed rough pasture disappeared. However in 1873 there were 2.5 million acres of common land remaining in Britain although there was little in Warwickshire probably because commons were generally enclosed to discourage squatters. One consequence of enclosure was that quite often part of the common land was set aside as allotments. This was regularised by the Allotments Act 1882 which required charities which owned land to release some of it as allotments. The final enclosures led to further loss of woodland and wilderness although the fields of the later enclosures were generally marked with hawthorn hedges. The later enclosed fields were typically around 10 to 20 acres in size.

Enclosures at this time occurred throughout the county from areas of Birmingham and Hampton-on-the-Hill in 1802 to Armscote in 1862, Blackwell in 1864, Baxterley in 1866, Whitchurch in 1867 and parts of Coventry in 1874.

Birmingham Commons to South, 1831	Leek Wootton, 1821
Baxterley, 1866	Milverton, 1805
Bedworth,1864	Morton Bagot, 1806
Bickenhill, Little Packington and Diddington, 1824	Morton Bagot, 1807
Birdingbury and Marton, 1802	Nether Whitacre, 1835
Birmingham, 1802	Norton Lindsey or Upper Norton, 1809
Corley (Corley Moor), 1847	Over Whitacre, 1822
Coventry (Waste Lands), 1874	Packwood, 1817
Coventry, 1859	Rowington and Old Stratford, 1824
Erdington and Witton, 1804	Sheldon, 1813
Exhall, 1840	Shipston-on-Stour, 1812
Glascote and Bolehall, 1809	Shuttington, 1804
Grandborough (Woolscott), 1858	Studley, 1824
Hampton-in-Arden (Balsall), 1802	Tanworth-in-Arden, 1857
Hampton-in-Arden, 1812,	Tredington (Armscote), 1862
Hartshill and Ansley, 1808	Tredington (Blackwell), 1864
Hatton, Haseley and Wroxhall, 1834	Tredington (Darlingscott), 1846
Kingsbury (Cliff and Bodymore Heath), 1855	Tredington (Newbold-on-Stour), 1849
Kingsbury (Hurley), 1822	Whitchurch, 1867
Lapworth and Rowington (Kingswood), 1808	Whitnash, 1849
	Wishaw, 1839
	Wolverton, 1826

Fig 63. Some Enclosures in the Nineteenth Century

There is a virtually complete run of distinctive regular rectangular fields from Temple Balsall to Shrewley which was created under these later enclosures. In Alcester the ridge and furrow in the fields was levelled by the Marquis of Hertford of Ragley Hall in 1813 so that no features remain visible today. The hamlet of Morton Bagot was enclosed in 1807 and there was no common land left. Morton Common in the parish was still waste at this time.

115

The main centres in this hamlet were at Meer Green, Church Green, Warnap, Greenhill Green and Morton Common.

Life on the farm was very varied during this century. From 1815 agriculture and the food chain in Britain was in chaos mainly because Napoleon prevented food imports and this action was unfortunately accompanied by a poor harvest. The Corn Laws were brought in to protect the incomes of farmers in 1815 but were repealed again in 1846 to further the cause of free trade. As well as the upsets caused by the enclosures there were many other highlights. The years from 1855 to 1875 made up two decades of great agricultural prosperity. There was an agricultural depression from the later 1870s because there was unrestricted competition and cereal prices fell as cheap grain was imported from the USA and Canada. In some places the use of the land was changed as, for example, in the Vale of Evesham where a vast area was turned over from grain production to market gardening. This depression in farming continued until 1900 and many more people moved from the country to the towns yet again. A little later in the winter of 1879-1880 there was excessive rainfall which was followed by an outbreak of sheep-rot and there was general distress.

Mechanisation of agriculture developed apace from the early nineteenth century and with larger fields and regional specialisation the productivity of the land was high. This development meant that lanes were sometimes blocked with steam traction engines, threshing boxes, living caravans and grain elevators. As part of the agricultural revolution there was also improved livestock breeding, better drainage and skilled grassland management. Extensive farm building also took place with the construction of barns, animal sheds, stables and dairies being common. A typical farm built in the early nineteenth century farm was brick built and isolated. James Smith of the cotton mill at Deanston near Stirling in Scotland was the father of modern drainage of agricultural land and his methods were soon widely adopted.

The area of land devoted to agriculture reached a peak in this century; it has been estimated that there was less woodland in 1895 than there was in 1966. With growing markets sheep pasture was converted back to cereal production and much of the century was also very profitable for dairy and cheese production. Farms tended to grow in size and in the nineteenth century many large estates were reorganised with a reduction in the number of tenants. In Coleshill the period from 1850 to 1873 was remembered as a time of 'High Farming' because of the expansion of the market for food in Birmingham and the repeal of the Corn Laws in 1846. On a national note the Royal Agricultural Society was founded in 1838 to advance the practice of agriculture.

Estates and Parks

Following the increase in wealth arising from improved farming and the success of the industrial revolution more and more large houses with generously sized estates were built in the county. A List of 58 Country Houses built in the county in the nineteenth century is shown in Fig 64.

Ashorne Hill House, Ashorne	Holloway House, Bidford
Attleborough Hall, Attleborough	Hurdle Hall, Bickenhill
Baraset, Alveston	Hurst House, Wootton Wawen
Barford Hill House, Barford	Ivy Hall, Solihull
Bilton Grange, Dunchurch	Knowle Hall new, Knowle
Bitham Hall, Avon Dassett	Light Hall, Tanworth
Blabers Hall, Fillongley	Limestone Hall, Church Lawford
Brailes House, Brailes	Ling Hall, Church Lawford
Brandon Hall, Brandon	Loxley Hall, Loxley
Brownsover Hall, Rugby	Malvern Hall, Leamington Hastings
Caldecote Hall, Caldecote	Moat House, Berkswell
Chadwick Manor, Chadwick End	Moat House, Fillongley
Clay Hall, Bickmarsh	Moat House, Walsgrave
Coleshill Hall, Coleshill	Packsaddle Hall, Fillongley
Dial House, Ashow	Ram Hall, Berkswell
Dingle House, Tanworth	Rookery Hall, Church Lawford
Edstone Hall, Bearley	Sandull House, Rowington
Ettington Park, Ettington	Shrubland House, Leamington
Fillongley Hall, Fillongley	Sparrow Hall, Combe Fields
Fillongley Hall, Fillongley	Springfield Hall, Knowle
Frog Hall, Burton Dassett	Springfield House, Ansley
Germany House, Bulkington	Springfield House, Bedworth
Gibraltar House, Leamington Hastings	Squab Hall, Bishops Tachbrook
Gipsy Hall, Aston Cantlow	Starve Hill, Claverdon
Great Alne Manor, Great Alne	Stone House, Allesley
Grove House, Coundon	Studley Castle, Studley
Hampton Manor. Hampton in Arden	Temple Grafton Court, Temple Grafton
Haseley Manor, Hatton	Tolldish Hall, Foleshill
Holbrook Grange, Little Lawford	Upper Skilts, Studley

Fig 64. List of Country Houses Built in the Nineteenth Century

There were some very impressive estates constructed in this century and it is said that the best oak trees in Warwickshire were on the Merevale Hall and Ragley Hall estates around 1813. In 1858 the park of Aston Hall in Birmingham still covered a large area.

Industrial Revolution, Mining, Factories

Fig 65. A symbolic winding wheel at the site of Keresley Colliery

This was the century in which the industrial revolution reinvented the economy of this country and was directly responsible for reshaping the appearance of some of the countryside. Stories were written about the 13 miles of fire and smoke between Birmingham and Wolverhampton and in 1832 J M W Turner painted the view of smoke and flames at Dudley which captures the appearance of many of the Black Country towns at this time. The number of industries which developed would have been bewildering to people from the previous century. They included cement works, power stations, electricity pylons, needle making (in the Arrow valley), brick making (especially near the Warwickshire coalfield around Coventry and Arden), and copper and brass manufacture on a large scale in Birmingham and the surrounding towns.

Fig 66. Miners' cottages at Piccadilly near Kingsbury.
An isolated street of apparently comfortable houses

Alcester was home to 15 needle works in the nineteenth century together with a mill, two malt-houses, a brewery and a gas works. There was also a rope walk because hemp was still grown in Alcester and the town had a rope maker. The enclosure in Long Compton in 1812 recorded two quarries at South Down Common and Kingstone Common which provided material for road improvements and maintenance. Weaving was still important in Bedworth in 1840 when there was a boom and up to 40% of homes in the town were involved in the trade in some way.

A major trade in Coventry and Nuneaton was ribbon making which was carried out in homes and factories. However in 1860 the duty on French and Swiss ribbons was abolished while the USA raised the duty for imports and the trade was destroyed virtually overnight. Coventry was soon a home for precision engineering and in 1861 population the population was 41,638, of which 25,000 were weavers and 2,500 were watchmakers. Coventry also made sewing machines and cycles and in the 1890s there were 40,000 people working

119

in the cycle trade. This was followed in 1895 by the start of the motor industry in the city, a mere vestige of which survives in 2009.

Coal mining went deeper below the surface of the earth as machinery improved and in the Arden area there were many north Warwickshire pit villages including Alvecote colliery from 1848 to 1965, Dordon mines dating from 1860, Birch Coppice colliery from 1875 with the deepest shaft of 1400 ft and Kingsbury colliery from 1894. Baddesley colliery had a new shaft in 1896, Newdigate colliery began in 1898 and Haunchwood & Griff collieries went deeper towards the end of the century. In 1840 25% of the population in the Bedworth area was employed in the mining industry and housed in low grade housing in suburbs which spread ever further into the countryside. Coal replaced water as a source of power for machinery and water and wind mills very soon fell into disuse. The consequences of this were smoky factories and dirty homes. Bedworth, for example, was described by the Reverend Bellairs as 'Black Bedworth'. In addition to coal there was mining of manganese ore on a major scale at Hayes Wood from 1820 until 1860 when the lodes ran out.

In the past manufacturing had often been carried out at home or in a workshop attached to the home but this century saw the rapid evolution of larger and more distant factories. In Kineton the corn mill was converted to steam. Also in Kineton the gas works was built in Warwick Road in 1863. Strangely the town does not have a mains gas supply today. The 1841 census shows that in the village of Stretton-on-Dunsmore in addition to the many farmers there were numerous craftsmen including three wheelwrights, three blacksmiths, several carpenters, two bricklayers, a plumber, a cooper, three shoemakers, four tailors, two dressmakers, a cattle dealer, one excise officer and a surgeon. In Hartshill lime trees were grown so that the wood could be used to fashion blocks around which felt hats were shaped. A totally different incursion into the countryside was made by a military village which was built in Budbrooke near Warwick in 1877. A lengthy tongue of development soon extended from Birmingham along the canal and railway towards Warwick.

L T C Rolt wrote that when the economist ousted the craftsman as the arbiter of the work he killed the goose which had once laid the eggs of pure gold.

Railways, Roads, Trams

Railways were developed at an astonishing rate in the nineteenth century and soon put paid to the commercial viability of most canals. The railways began around 1825 and a horse-drawn tramway was built from Stratford to Moreton in Marsh in the very earliest times. This tramway received an act of parliament in 1821 and was opened in 1826. The branch of the Stratford-Moreton Tramway to Shipston-on-Stour was opened in 1836 and the main line of the tramway was straightened in 1889. An anonymous poem was written about the tramway –

To see our iron railway
It makes our heart content,
To know what's saved in firing
Will nearly pay the rent

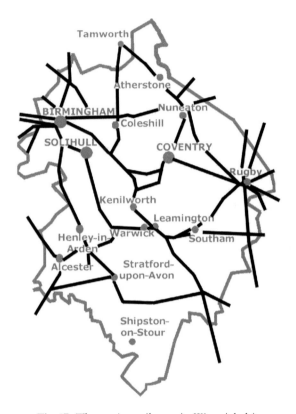

Fig 67. The major railways in Warwickshire

The major railway line from London to Birmingham was opened in 1838 with the terminus at Curzon Street and Rugby and Coventry were on this line. The equivalent of the Euston Arch still survives in Birmingham at Curzon Street. On a less ambitious scale the line from Leamington to Rugby opened in 1851. The first railway branch line came to Kineton in 1871 followed by a line to Stratford-upon-Avon in 1873. In Alcester the railway came in 1866 providing a link to the north to Birmingham and south to Evesham. In 1876 the railway was

121

built to Bearley junction. Some previously insignificant villages were provided with stations and developed accordingly. This improvement in transport reduced the isolation of many villages deep in the country and Rugby rapidly became a railway town with lines radiating to nine directions.

The enclosures had some impact on the specification and routing of roads. For example, in the enclosure documents for Norton Lindsey in 1809 the widths of the roads were specified. Warwick Road was to be 40 feet wide, Snitterfield and Hatton roads were to be 30 feet, the bridleway to Sherborne was to be 15 feet and the footpaths 6 feet wide.

Alongside the growth of the railways the establishment of turnpike trusts continued in this century and eventually 20,000 miles of roads in Britain were run by trusts. The turnpike from Kineton to Southam began in 1852 and tollhouses still exist at Kineton and Gaydon. There was a tollhouse between Haselor and Temple Grafton. The Alcester to Wootton Wawen turnpike was established in 1814. All the existing turnpike trusts ended in 1895 when district and borough councils took over responsibility for the roads. Like many other roads the Fosse Way near Chesterton was a gated road at this time. At the very end of the century the nascent motor car was preparing to present new challenges to the road builder and those charged with maintaining them.

Trams were another hybrid form of transport introduced at this time and the system through the rural gap between Warwick to Leamington Spa lasted from 1882 to 1930; trams were initially horse-drawn but the route was electrified in 1905. There was also an extensive tram system in Coventry which was begun in 1884 and was initially operated by steam trams. It extended as far as Stoke, Earlsdon and Bell Green and through the country to Bedworth. Trams never ran in the city again after the damage caused in the Blitz in November 1940. Birmingham also started with horse trams from 1872, followed by steam trams in 1882, and the system was electrified in 1901. At its peak the Birmingham trams had 70 miles of routes running to such places as Acocks Green, West Bromwich and Dudley and the last routes were not closed until 1953.

In 1840 the market closed at Kineton because the improvement in roads enabled ready access to markets in other towns. The Market House was demolished in 1892 and replaced by a school in the centre of the Market Square.

Building, Growth of Towns,
Country Houses Abandoned

Oversley Castle was built in the early nineteenth century at the suggestion of the future George IV to improve the view from Ragley Hall. At Wixford the hut in the corner of the churchyard was built for the rector's horse and there was a small school at Morton Bagot for a few years in this century.

Fig 68. The ruins of Guy's Cliffe House, near Warwick

We have seen that increasing industrialisation led to many people moving from the countryside to the villages and towns. This century is a story of the rapid spread of many of these settlements, gobbling up many acres of countryside in the process.

Many towns became very overcrowded because new building did not keep pace with the influx of people and the people could not afford the housing which was available. The overcrowding was a serious hazard to health and public health measures were taken later in the century to improve conditions. This was followed in the next century by much overdue slum clearance. The stories of families of seven or more people living and sleeping in two small rooms are reminders of the conditions seen in some townships in Africa today. Examples of these 'back-to-backs' are preserved by the National Trust in Birmingham. In the nineteenth century Coventry was still largely confined within the walls built in 1400 and was seriously overcrowded. The provision of clean water and effective rubbish and sewage removal were at the top of the list of jobs for local councils to attend to. As a first step many village water pumps were provided in this century.

KEY

to 1810
to 1820
to 1830
to 1845
to 1890
to 1920
to 1970
to 2009

SCALE

2 kilometres

Fig 69. Diagram of the rapid growth of Royal Leamington Spa
from a small hamlet, Leamington Priors. The white area is open space

Leamington Spa was a special case in that the town spread rapidly in all directions from its centre in Bath Street and Clemens Street as the popularity of the spring waters grew, tourism and residents increased and tradesmen moved into town to service the needs of the residents. For example a one acre site was sold in 1809 for the construction of Gloucester Street which leads off Bath Street and the Jephson Gardens were begun in 1834.

The model village of Bournville was built on the outskirts of Birmingham from 1878 to 1906 to an original plan to house the workers at the chocolate factory. It followed the example set by Thomas Salt at Saltaire in West Yorkshire from 1850 and the later development in Port Sunlight on Merseyside which was begun in 1888 by Lord Lever. These towns were built on green field sites and included all the facilities required by the residents such as churches, schools and hospitals (but not public houses).

Fig 70. The oldest cottages surviving in Church Street in Leamington Spa

Nuneaton eventually burst out of its medieval boundaries with many new terraces of houses being built. In 1848 the town was in a very poor state and it was not until the 1890s that houses of superior character were built and the suburbs arrived. Many estates were built in Nuneaton in the century including Attleborough Road, Croft Road, Edward Street, the estates in Attleborough, and the Edward Street area of Coton together with the main estates round Abbey Green and either side of Queens Road. Manor Court Road became the centre of a new suburb with imposing houses being built around 1870. In 1893 the Manor Hospital was built. The Priory in Nuneaton was rebuilt from 1876 as the Abbey Church.

Mining villages were built in this century at Galley Common, Ansley Common and later at New Arley. In the same vicinity Griff House in Bedworth was the residence of George Eliot but in 1841 she decided to move to Bird Grove in Foleshill in the countryside near to Coventry. Even in a rural village like Studley in the south of the county the growth of the needle industry led to the creation of semi-urban slums.

The owners of Baddesley Clinton house became impecunious in this century and, unlike more wealthy contemporaries, could not afford to significantly update it; the house remains as a largely fifteenth century building now owned by the National Trust. Aston Hall was bought by Birmingham City Council in 1864 as a place of entertainment when the owner died.

At Hampton Lucy most of the old cottages were demolished in the mid nineteenth century and they were not rebuilt because there were not enough jobs for the residents. Similarly in Kinwarton many cottages and farmhouses were demolished in the mid nineteenth century and only the church, rectory, glebe farm and six cottages remained along with a dovecote which is now cared for by the National Trust. However in Henley-in-Arden many buildings from before 1840 survive including many seventeenth century timber framed buildings. At this time Henley-in-Arden had a courthouse, a post office, doctors' surgeries, private schools, a mental hospital, many inns and banks and estate agents.

Villages Rebuilt, Hospitals, Schools

In the nineteenth century a number of villages were largely rebuilt including Alderminster, Wimpstone, Preston-on-Stour and Combrook, which replaced the village of Compton Verney when the house was built. There are estate cottages at Charlecote from this time and estate villages were also built at Walton, Sherbourne and at Alscot Park at Alderminster. There were also many and varied building projects in this period. Studley Castle was built in 1854. Kennels for the Warwickshire Hunt were built in Kineton in 1839 and at Morton Bagot a home for the destitute was built on the common.

The Convent of Poor Clares Coletinnes was built in 1870 at Baddesley Clinton and much later starred in an Alan Whicker TV documentary. In this century the wave of Shakespeare pilgrims to Stratford-upon-Avon began. The Weston-under-Wetherley hospital was built as boys reformatory in 1840. Chesterton School had space for 40 children in 1866. Also in Chesterton, the Manor was demolished 1802 and the stables became Humble Bee Cottages.

126

Churches Modernised

Fig 71. Lower Shuckburgh, an unusual church in a Moorish style

This was a century in which the money was available to refurbish many churches and we can still benefit from many of these beautiful buildings. It is impossible to note more than a few of these churches. For example the village of Wappenbury has two churches, one Roman Catholic designed by Pugin and the Anglican church. Lower Shuckburgh church was rebuilt in 1864 and is unique in having distinctly Moorish influences. However the church in Radway was demolished in 1865 and rebuilt on another site nearby and there is also a Primitive Methodist chapel built in 1866. The Radway Society of Friends had a meeting house until it became Oriel Cottage in 1851. There is also a chapel at Knightcote. Little Compton church was rebuilt 1863 and Chesterton church was restored in 1862 after falling into disrepair. At Hampton Lucy the church was rebuilt in Early English style in 1826 and the nearby church at Charlecote received the same treatment in 1851.

127

End of Feudalism, Population Expansion,
Joseph Arch

An ironic ditty quoted by Charles Dickens in 1844 on the social system summarises the position at the beginning of the nineteenth century -

"O let us love our occupations,
Bless the squire and his relations,
Live upon our daily rations,
And always know our proper stations."
Charles Dickens, The Chimes, Second Quarter (1844).

The situation was to change rapidly in the next 100 years.

There was a huge growth in population in the nineteenth century; from 1800 the population of Britain more than trebled from about 9 million to 32.5 million by 1900. This was despite diseases which were rampant at various times in the century. For example Bedworth lost 60 people to smallpox in 1825, 26 to cholera in 1832 and 106 to smallpox in 1845. Despite this the population of the town rose from 3,161 in 1801 to 5,059 in 1851. Even in Chesterton there were outbreaks of diphtheria and measles in 1814 and 1815 when 11 children died.

The population of Coventry in 1801 was 21,853 and in the 1901 census it was 88,107. The population of Nuneaton increased at a great rate from 5,135 in 1851 to 24,996 in 1901. This increased population was squeezed into much the same area of land which became known as the Nuneaton and Chilvers Coton Urban District Council in 1893.

The early nineteenth century was a very hard time with real starvation and wage demands which were not met. Unemployment followed the Napoleonic Wars in 1815 and unrest began as farm workers were displaced and farm machinery was smashed. There was further unrest in protest at the mechanisation of industry in 1830 with rick-burning led by Captain Swing, a pseudonym for an anonymous leader in the south of the country. At this date about 300,000 of 686,000 rural families in Britain were on poor relief. A local man, Joseph Arch, formed the National Agricultural Workers Union following his speech at the Stags Head at Wellesbourne in 1872. He later became an MP and, to some extent, lost the confidence of the agricultural workers he represented. There is now a pub named after him in Barford, his birthplace. He wrote in his autobiography –

"There was only one remedy, and that was Combination. The men were weak, if they would be strong they must unite. I saw the day drawing steadily nearer and nearer,

when the wretched units of labour would be forced to unite, driven to combine. I saw the time surely coming when, as one man, they would waken to the fact that 'Union makes Strength'."

There was a massive change in the appearance of the countryside from 1850 as the majority of the population had moved to the towns, as agriculture developed to feed the increasing population and as waste land disappeared.

Other snippets of information may be of interest. It is notable that most of the ecclesiastical parish boundaries in the first half of nineteenth century could be traced to early medieval times. As well as working hard people also had time for entertainment and the first stand was built at Warwick racecourse in 1809.

Landscape Conservation is Invented

As the countryside was subjected to unparalleled change there was growing concern about the loss of what was valued from the past and the beauty and characteristics of the historic landscapes. In 1865 the Commons, Open Spaces and Footpaths Preservation Society was formed and it still exists today under the shortened name of the Open Spaces Society. The John Ruskin Guild of St George was formed in 1871 to buy land and preserve it in accordance with the Code of the Guild. The Lake District Defence Society was formed in 1883; this society was renamed The Friends of the Lake District and is now a branch of the Campaign to Protect Rural England. The National Trust was founded in 1895 with the aim of preserving land and buildings at a particular stage in their development; it now owns 1% of the land in England and Wales. One of the founders of the National Trust, Octavia Hill, said

"It would seem well that some portion of the Wealds should be kept for the enjoyment, refreshment and rest of those who have no country house, but who need, from time to time, this outlook over the fair land which is their inheritance as Englishmen".

Public concern about the protection of the countryside was so great that parliament began to bring into law new legislation to protect features of the landscape. The tension between future economic growth and the future of the environment which became apparent in the nineteenth century has become increasingly high profile until the present day and the process of law making has continued at an ever increasing pace. The first of the legislation was the Open Spaces Act of 1877 which set out to preserve open spaces in towns throughout the land. The concern was not restricted to Britain and there was worldwide growth of concern about historic landscapes. This was demonstrated by the establishment of the first national park in the world in 1864 in the USA at Yosemite Park.

Chapter Fourteen

1900 to 1918

Introduction

The Edwardian period was, in some ways, a time of mild anti-climax following the period of national self-confidence and development which typified the reign of Queen Victoria. However there were many inventions and innovations relating to the countryside which were developed during the period including the infant internal combustion engine, agricultural chemicals, improved selective stock breeding and processed animal feeds.

Fig 72. Deer at Charlecote Park

Tractors, Cheap Food Imports,
Expansion of Towns

At the start of the century the land was still being ploughed mainly with horses and stationary steam engines because the first tractors which were built were very heavy and easily became bogged down in the fields. Many hedges were grubbed up to make the work of these steam engines easier. The firm of Bomford and Evershed at Salford Priors was a large agricultural contractor in

131

the south of the county from around 1904. The last plough pulled by oxen was reputedly used in Sussex in 1914 but horses continued to be used for many years for ploughing and other agricultural purposes.

This was a time of increasing imports of cheap food but, nevertheless, the Vale of Evesham had 10,000 acres of market gardens spreading into Warwickshire along the Avon valley. This business sector was in danger of decline and the Warwickshire and Worcestershire County Councils provided financial aid to owners in the period from 1900 to 1913.

Expansion of industry and housing continued to encroach on the countryside. During this period 500,000 acres of land were lost from agriculture in Britain in 15 years. Increasing industrialisation continued to attract people to come to live and work in towns for a better standard of living. Nationally the number of farm labourers fell by 36% between 1870 and 1914. The Development Commission was established in 1909 by David Lloyd George to combat decades of agricultural depression and it survived through various changes until 1988. There was also an increase in the organisation of agriculture with the founding of the Country Landowners Organisation in 1907 and the establishment of the National Farmers Union in 1908 as very successful lobby groups for farmers and both of them were active in Warwickshire from the earliest days.

Electricity, Telephones,
Railway is King, Growth of the Car

Life was eased by the growing availability of electricity and telephones in urban areas. Unfortunately it was also the beginning of a century of increasing pollution. This was part of the period when the railway was the king of transport systems. No new railways were built in the county during this time but some new freight depots were constructed. The structure and maintenance of roads improved slowly as the design of the internal combustion engine and the production of road vehicles developed but no major roads were built in the county in this period.

Mass production developed and many of the backyard workshops of Birmingham closed around the turn of the century as demand and prices fell for their wares. A number of iconic buildings such as Fort Dunlop were built by the healthy new industries. However many original early weaving cottage factories had survived at Kingfield in Radford, Coventry, at this time. Coventry was very dependent on the road transport industries as there were 73 car makers and 78 cycle makers in Coventry by 1910. The Stoke Heath industrial estate and the aerodrome at Radford were built in Coventry at this time and the Whitmore Park plant in north of the city manufactured munitions. Reservoirs continued to be built to improve water supply.

132

The Housing Problem, More Country Houses

The population continued to grow apace as did the movement of people from the country to the town. Overcrowding in towns continued to be a serious problem to the health and welfare of residents. Towns became bigger and swallowed up necklaces of the countryside around them. The population of Bedworth in 1901 was 7,169 and Nuneaton became a borough in 1907.

Fig 73. Moreton Hall before the disastrous fire in 2008

The Housing & Town Planning Act 1909 was the first act which aimed to control the design and size of new housing and heralded mass council housing after private rental became less common.

Dunchurch Lodge, Dunchurch	Moreton Paddox, Moreton Morrell
Moreton Hall, Moreton Morrell	Slateley Hall, Kingsbury

Fig 74. Country houses built in the early years of the twentieth century

Airfields, Street Advertisements

The new world of flying soon had an impact on Warwickshire. Lilbourne airfield just over the border in Leicestershire was established in 1915 and this was followed by Radford airfield in Coventry in 1917 but there are no surviving
133

buildings. There were landing fields at Meriden and Knowle from 1918. The most significant development in this period was the establishment of Whitley airfield at Coventry in 1918 and this was bought by Armstrong Whitworth in 1920 for the construction of aircraft. However production moved from Whitley to Baginton in 1936. Castle Bromwich airfield started 1912 and it was taken over by the Royal Flying Corps in 1915 and became a civil airfield from 1918. There are no surviving buildings.

Street advertisements for a multitude of products were uncontrolled until this time when the Control of Advertisements Acts was introduced in 1907. Also around this time village halls became a common feature as a focus of village life. This was the Edwardian Age when many of the aristocracy are often reputed to have thrived. However a number of hereditary property owners found it difficult to maintain their country houses and Moor Hall at Sutton Coldfield was demolished in 1905 and also Erdington Hall in 1912.

Chapter Fifteen

Between the Wars
1918 to 1939

**Agriculture in Decline, More Mechanisation of Agriculture,
Country Estates in Decline**

The concentration of Britain on industrial development in this period meant that there was less attention paid to the performance of the agricultural industry and by 1939 only 30% of the country's food requirements were being produced in the UK. The result was that in the 1930s farming was in the doldrums and there was little political awareness of the fact before the war began. This failing was attended to urgently during the second world war and agricultural output increased significantly in the UK and, of course, in Warwickshire.

Improvements in metal working, and production in general, and the development of tractors and agricultural machinery in particular, led to the production of large, efficient ploughs and other implements. It is estimated that there were 60,000 tractors in Britain by 1938 and in the same year the first combine harvesters were seen. Yet again larger fields were created by grubbing up hedges to make the best use of these new ploughs and this is a process that continued into the 1990s.

The destruction of woods and forests continued into the twentieth century and this resulted in a severe lack of timber. The Forestry Commission was created in 1919 and introduced controls on the cutting down of trees as well as planting them in this period.

Between the wars many country estates were broken up and from the 1920s a number of country houses and traditional farm buildings were left to become derelict. For example in 1919 the Long Compton estate was sold by the Marquess of Northampton and split up; it comprised 1,850 acres, seven farms, a water mill, allotments, the Red Lion Hotel in the village and 73 cottages. Land around Sydenham in Leamington Spa was converted from farm fields to use as allotments from 1933.

Industrial Growth, Road Congestion,
More Airfields, Railway Closures

This was another period during which there was a great increase in industrial production. Coventry continued to be a centre for the motor car industry with mergers of the smaller manufacturers and major car plants were built for Rootes and Standard on virgin countryside. The major plant for Rootes was built at Ryton-on-Dunsmore under the shadow factory scheme. British Thomson Houston (BTH) established an electrical equipment factory in Coventry and a plastics works was opened at Tyseley. The 'B' station at Hams Hall power station was built in 1937 further extending into the countryside. The national electricity grid was established in 1925 and pylons became a prominent feature of the landscape. Pylons caused similar concerns at this time to those provoked by mobile telephone masts and wind farms today. Electricity arrived in rural villages such as Kineton in the 1920s.

Fig 75. View from Chesterton

In the 1930s there were problems with congestion on many roads including the A5 Watling Street, A38, A45 and A34 trunk roads which carved their way through Warwickshire. There were conflicts in the process of deciding national policy as highway engineers wanted 2,899 miles of motorway to be built but the association of county transport engineers only wanted 1,000 miles. The first dual carriageway in Britain was opened in 1925 at the London end of the Great West Road. The city of Birmingham was near to gridlock in the 1930s but, to some

136

extent, the situation was saved by the approaching wartime restrictions and the shortage and rationing of fuel.

There were developments in aviation as Baginton airfield was cut out of the countryside in 1935. There was also a private landing ground at Woodley House in Kineton and one building survives; also there was Bonniksen's private landing ground to the south of Leamington. There were other private landing grounds at Milcote Hall near Stratford-upon-Avon and at Lawford Heath. The municipal civil airport at Elmdon (Birmingham) was opened in 1939 but it was converted to military use almost immediately.

The railway from Shipston-on-Stour to Moreton-in-Marsh closed in 1929 and that from Alcester to Bearley in 1939 along with station closures at Shipston-on-Stour in 1929 and Bulkington in 1931.

Housing for Heroes, Suburbanisation, Ribbon Development, Green Belt

The Housing & Town Planning Act of 1919 set the scene for the building of mass council housing to provide homes for the heroes of the Great War. 213,000 houses were built in Britain. In addition in the 1920s & 1930s vast private estates were built on the edges of towns and between 1930 and 1940 a total of 2.7 million houses were built in Britain in a very piecemeal pattern across the countryside. The Town and Country Planning Act 1932 was intended to stop this flood of development by requiring that local authorities for towns with over 20,000 population should have a proper legally enforced plan for future development.

As road and rail transport improved there was a significant trend towards suburbanisation and more countryside disappeared beneath houses and roads. 100,000 homes were built in Birmingham alone between 1926 and 1940. In the period 1918 to 1939 the number of houses in Britain increased by a huge 50% and an average of 62,000 acres (25,100 hectares) of land per year were lost to housing. In the 1930s there was a trend towards lower density housing which increased yet further the area of land used. An absurd fact is that by 1937 enough land had been allocated to cater for a population seven times the existing number of residents. The allocation was for 291 million people when the population of England was only around 39 million and this was despite the fact that in the decade of the 1930s there was, in fact, a net migration of people out of Britain.

Ribbon development on roads leading out of Nuneaton and other local towns before 1935 reflected a national trend which had been highlighted by the Council for the Preservation of Rural England (CPRE) in 1926. Under the Restriction of Ribbon Development Act 1935 development was restricted within

220 feet of the centre of all existing classified roads and on other roads designated by the Minister. This meant that the building of homes and businesses alongside roads leading out of towns was prohibited. Many of the towns in Warwickshire have development dating prior to 1935 alongside the road with infilling at a later date behind. CPRE at this time also backed campaigns for national parks and areas of outstanding natural beauty to be established.

Fig 76. An ornamental signpost at Norton Lindsey, recently restored

Plans for mass building in Lillington to the north of Leamington were approved in 1927. Bedworth and Bulkington spread rapidly and became joined together in 1938. Council houses were built in King Johns Road in Kineton in this period and 1,519 council houses were built in Nuneaton by 1939 along with 3,483 private houses in Weddington. In Coventry slum clearance began in the 1920s and hundreds of historic buildings over 200 years old were destroyed and also many streets were widened in the city at this time. It could be argued that the destruction of the past in Coventry in the 1920s was greater than was achieved by the blitz of 1940.

Also in this period the concept of the Green Belt was first properly established by the London and Home Counties Act 1938 and in 1939 there was a plan for the first West Midlands Green Belt to control the ambitions for the Birmingham conurbation to expand.

Urban Growth

In this period before the war Coventry was reputed to be a fine city said to be *"like thick butter spread over a layer of medievalism"*. Industry was thriving and the city centre was a pleasing mix of old and new. St Michael's church in Coventry became a cathedral in 1918 and shortly after this in 1922 the old barracks area was converted into a market. Unfortunately in Nuneaton the end of the First World War in 1918 was followed by 20 years of depression. Despite the massive growth in earlier years the population of Nuneaton only increased from 42,104 in 1921 to 46,521 in 1931. In 1932 Weddington and Caldecote were added to the existing borough of Nuneaton. In 1921 the population of Bedworth in the north increased to 11,548 while the population of Kineton in the south reached 1,000.

Construction of the landmark Rugby radio station commenced in January 1926 but it has now almost disappeared. The well-known point to point races at Chesterton finished in 1939 although some events were organized after the war.

Conservation, Planning Arrives

A major incident in England in this period was an invasion of Kinder Scout in the Peak District on 24th April 1932 by walkers who were demanding the right to roam throughout the countryside. This right was eventually achieved and this meant that landowners, including those in Warwickshire, had to allow public access to some previously restricted areas. This right of access was eventually enshrined in the National Parks and Access to the Countryside Act 1949.

The movement to protect the countryside was growing and, amongst others, the famous historian GM Trevelyan made a number pronouncements.

He said that *"without vision the people perish and without sight of the beauty of nature the spiritual power of the British people will be stifled"*.

Trevelyan also wrote at this time that *"with shorter hours of work, holidays with pay, and increasing leisure for millions has become a national problem and it makes the provision of National Parks increasingly and urgently necessary"*.

Trevelyan also noted that *"we are daily permitting, and by our laws encouraging, the destruction of the regions that people desire"*.

HV Morton wrote in his book 'In Search of England' *"Never before have so many people been searching for England"* and the Prime Minister himself, Stanley Baldwin, pronounced *"To me England is the country and the country is England"*.

About 70% of the country houses in England changed ownership between 1870 and 1937 as inherited wealth was taxed or spent and newly affluent people wanted to buy into the country life.

The Town and Country Planning Act 1932 extended the designation of usage to all land. This meant that plans had to be drawn up which showed the purposes for which all land could be used. Most land was naturally allocated for agriculture and other uses including for housing, various classes of businesses, open spaces and recreation.

Chapter Sixteen

World War II

Food Shortages and Rationing,
Planning for the Peace

When the war began in 1939 only 30% of the food that was needed was produced within the UK. Consequently there were intensive efforts to strive for self sufficiency during and after the war. This had a major impact on the countryside as woodland was destroyed to provide more land for food production and hedges were pulled out to make bigger fields. The project coined a number of slogans including 'Dig for Victory' and 'Every Acre Counts'. History shows that war is nearly always good news for farmers because there is little competition from imports of food. A Government Machinery Depot was established at Atherstone to coordinate farming during World War II. The concentration on bringing more land into production led to the loss of wide areas of traditional moors, heaths and woodland throughout the country.

The prospects of reconstruction after World War II led to a great national interest in planning and development. Starting in the middle of the War the government set up a number of commissions which were to have a major impact on planning and the future of the countryside for the whole country including Warwickshire. In 1942 the Scott Report was published on land utilisation in rural areas and a white paper was published in 1944. The second consideration was by the Barlow Commission in 1940 which was directed to look at the distribution of the industrial population to relieve economic depression. The Uthwatt Report of 1942 was the most influential and was concerned with choosing the most suitable land for a particular purpose and issues of compensation and fair allocation of increases in land values when development took place. It dealt with debates during wartime between rural preservationists and agricultural modernisers. The Labour Party supported the need to protect the look of the landscape as part of the nation's heritage and national identity, in line with public opinion at the time, but it also sought to encourage the physical planning of both town and country in a way that rejected some of the more anti-metropolitan tendencies of the rural preservationists. In addition there was the Dudley Report in 1944 on the design of dwellings. Taken together these reports led to the Town and Country Planning Act 1947 (see next chapter).

Fig 77. Airfields in Warwickshire

Industry Adapts to Wartime, Military Establishments,

Many peacetime factories were turned over to producing goods for the war effort. This applied particularly to factories in Coventry. In addition new factories known as 'shadow factories' were built which were intended to mirror the activities of another factory so that if one was destroyed production could continue at the other. One such factory was built on a green field site for Maudslay at Great Alne. In Warwickshire, as all over the country, the Second World War made use of unemployed people in depressed areas and women were also widely employed in wartime factories and labour was sucked from the countryside into the towns to aid the war effort.

142

The impacts of the war on the landscape in Warwickshire were many and various. Many defences and military establishments were built throughout the country and a surprising number were built in Warwickshire which could be thought to be distant from the war zones.

Fig 78. WWII hangar at Wellesbourne Mountford

Six defensive stop lines crossed Warwickshire and these were intended to impede the advance of any invading forces. These stop lines were along the Oxford Canal (Claydon to Warwick), along the River Avon (Bidford-on-Avon to Coventry), Napton to Coventry, Coventry to Tamworth, Stratford to Tamworth and from Droitwich to Watling Street utilising part of the Avon Line. The main structures which were built on the stop lines were pillboxes of various designs and anti-tank obstacles including concrete blocks, walls, horizontal and vertical rails and ditches. Pillboxes can be seen today along the canals at Napton, Clifton-on-Dunsmore, Priors Hardwick, Radford Semele and Warwick. Concrete blocks of hexagonal and cylindrical shape can be seen at various locations in the county including Fenny Compton, Willoughby, Braunston, Rugby, Old Arley, Devitts Green (where there is a collection of them in a garden) Fillongley, Maxstoke, Easenhall and Kingsbury.

A major part of the war effort was the construction of airfields and the re-use of existing airfields for military purposes. The main structures at the airfields were runways, control towers, pillboxes, technical and administration buildings, training blocks, domestic buildings and prefabricated huts. Most

143

airfields had three runways at 60 degrees and at least eight types of hangars were built. See the panel for further details. LTC (Tom) Rolt wrote in 'Clouded Mirror' that World War II airfields *"turned fertile fields into treeless steppes ruled with a rigid pattern of runways"*

Ansty airfield, 285 acres, was opened with grass runways in January 1936. The final use as a flying school ended in 1953. It was used as a factory site by Armstrong Siddeley from 1942 and is now an industrial park of 310 acres.

Birmingham (Elmdon), airfield (800 acres) was acquired by the city council in February 1936. It was taken over by the military in 1939 until the RAF left in June 1946. It is now the major civil airport in the region.

Bramcote airfield was constructed in 1939 and flying ceased in 1957 when it became a naval station called HMS Gamecock. It became Gamecock Barracks for the army and it continues in use today. Hangars still exist on the site.

Brinklow (at Bretford) airfield was a satellite landing ground from October 1941 until it closed in 1945. It has been returned to agricultural use.

Castle Bromwich airfield was founded before the first world war and It was requisitioned in August 1914. It was used for building aircraft. It was promoted as Birmingham airport in the 1920s. It was eventually sold in September 1960 and is now the huge Castle Vale housing estate.

Church Lawford airfield was constructed in 1940 and closed in 1955. It has been used for landfill and as an industrial estate.

Coventry (Baginton) airfield opened in 1936 and, like Castle Bromwich, was used for constructing aircraft but production ceased in 1965. The last active squadron left in 1943 and a passenger terminal was built in 1952 and civil use continues today. Hangars still exist from wartime.

Gaydon airfield was built in 1941 and was used until 1945. It reopened in 1954 as a V bomber base which closed in October 1974. It was bought by Rover and is now used by various motor companies. The Heritage Motor Museum is also on the site. Hangars and the control tower still exist.

Hockley Heath airfield was a relief landing ground from 1941 and closed in 1948. Hockley Heath was an airfield with grass runways and was used for relief landing. It is now used for farming.

Honiley airfield was built in 1940-1941 and closed in 1957. It is now owned by a motor vehicle development company and used for vehicle testing.

Leamington Spa, Bonniksens airfield at Harbury Lane in Bishops Tachbrook, was always in private hands and was used only as a relief landing ground during the war. It is now used for light industry.

Long Marston airfield was built 1940-1941 and was used by the RAF until 1954. It is now used by light aircraft and as an event venue.

Nuneaton (Lindley) airfield was a satellite to Bramcote. It was 4.5 miles NNE of Nuneaton between Higham on the Hill and Fenny Drayton.

Snitterfield airfield was built in 1942-1943 and closed in 1946. It is now used partly as a golf course, partly for gliding.

Southam Fields airfield, east of the village on Daventry Road, was a relief landing ground from 1940 to 1944. It is now used for farming.

Stratford (at Atherstone-on-Stour) airfield started 1940 as a satellite to Wellesbourne and it closed in November 1945. It has returned to agriculture. A hangar and the control tower still remain.

Warwick airfield was a relief landing ground which opened in December 1941. It closed at the end of 1945 and a blister hangar survived for many years as a landmark on Stratford Road.

Wellesbourne Mountford airfield opened in April 1941 and was sold in 1966. It is now part industry, part private airfield and flying school. An original hangar still remains.

Whitley Abbey airfield was not used in the war. It was set up in 1923 for the manufacture of aircraft and closed about 1934 when production moved to Baginton. It is now used for business purposes.

Wibtoft was a decoy airfield for Bramcote in World War II.

Fig 79. 19 airfield sites in Warwickshire

In addition to the airfields there were bombing ranges at Grandborough, Priors Hardwick, Shotteswell and Idlicote. As a consequence it is said that the village of Shotteswell suffered more from the RAF than from the Luftwaffe.

Airfield pillboxes remain at Long Marston, Stratford (Atherstone), Church Lawford, Bramcote, Baginton and Elmdon. Battle headquarters remain at Long Marston, Stratford, Wellesbourne, Baginton, Bramcote and Elmdon airfields. There were many anti-aircraft gun sites during the war. Most have disappeared but substantial remains are at Bannerhill near Kenilworth and Fillongley.

Perhaps a less known fact is that a number of decoy sites were set up in the county which were intended to distract bombers at night by appearing to be towns or airfields. There is a little remaining evidence of these decoys at Pillerton Priors, Hunningham and Bretford.

Fig 80. Disused military storage depot at Long Marston

Turning now to the Army, Budbrooke Barracks was established in 1940 as a training camp and was demolished in 1969 and some officers' houses remain in Montgomery Avenue. There are also the remains of a rifle range. Bramcote Gamecock barracks is still active and so is the Kineton ammunition depot which covered most of Battle Farm and Thistleton Farm. At Kineton there were 152 World War II explosive houses but only a few of those remain. Long Marston Depot which was largely used as stores was vacated in 1999. In addition soldiers were billeted at Walton Hall, Moreton Hall and Moreton Paddox. There were Czechoslovak Brigade Billets at Barford, Wellesbourne, Moreton Morrell, Kineton and Butlers Marston. There was a prisoner of war Camp at Ladbroke and some huts remain. There were also POW camps at Long Marston, Ettington, near Coleshill, Birdingbury, Merevale Hall, Arbury Hall, Kineton, Stoneleigh and Kenilworth. Elsewhere in the county a military hospital was built in Stoneleigh Park and this site is now a business park. Another military establishment was at Newbold Revel house which was occupied by the RAF in the war and is now used for Prison Service training.

The final reminders of wartime are the remains of air raid shelters. These were many and numerous. Examples remain to be seen at Southam, Clifton-on-Dunsmore, Abbey Fields in Kenilworth, Stratford (Atherstone) airfield, Long Marston airfield and Wellesbourne airfield.

A major impact of the war, of course, was damage caused by the attacks; the main impact was in Coventry where over 50,000 houses were destroyed or damaged, mostly in the blitz of November 1940. But it is often not recognized that throughout the war other pockets of damage were caused in the towns of Kenilworth, Leamington Spa, Lillington and Nuneaton (a total of 131 people were killed by enemy action in Nuneaton), as well as villages such as Weddington, Ryton-on-Dunsmore, Pailton and Dunchurch.

Fig 81. Pillbox alongside the canal at Napton

There were dangerous incidents in the countryside during the war such as at Temple Grafton when, in 1944, a plane crashed very close to the village after crew bailed out over Leamington and also the church tower at Whatcote was hit by a jettisoned bomb. Oldbury Hall was demolished in 1950 after being hit by an incendiary bomb in 1942. It is reputed that Idlicote House was used by Luftwaffe as a landmark because it was very light in appearance.

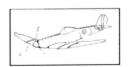

147

Chapter Seventeen

1945 to 1949

**Response to Food Shortages, Agriculture Support Payments,
Technology, Fertilisers, Pesticides**

Following the problems caused by food shortages in the war the main objective for agriculture in this decade was for the UK to become self-sufficient in food supply. It was also generally recognised that although the main purpose of the countryside was to produce food however there was going to be less land available for agriculture in the future as building development spread across the landscape. Grain yields per acre increased with improvements in agricultural methods and new crops such as flax and oilseed rape were widely grown. There were post-war incentives for farmers to buy new equipment, to reclaim marginal land and to maximise crop yields and land drainage was improved by digging deeper, wider ditches. More land was made usable and efficient to cultivate by grubbing out yet more hedges.

As we have noted agriculture was seen to be of strategic importance and this, ironically, quite quickly led to food surpluses and a reduction in the prices paid to farmers. The government had to introduce price guarantees for farmers under the 1947 Agriculture Act through 'deficiency payments'. As farming spread to less profitable land capital grants were made to certain groups, such as hill farmers, under the same legislation to encourage them to continue in business.

Artificial fertilisers were used much more intensively from this time. At one time it was roughly calculated that using twenty times the amount of fertilisers would double the yields. The problems created by this approach included the fact that fertilisers reduced diversity because they were quicker acting than manure and they also found their way into water sources affecting water supplies over a wide area. The productivity of agriculture was also accelerated by the use of pesticides as well as artificial fertilisers. The impact of these pesticides on health and the environment was little understood at the time. For example the insecticide DDT was widely used but is now accepted as being very harmful and was banned outright in 1978. There is still concern today about the legacy effects of DDT and whether they are reversible. An additional issue is that many insects have become immune to the effects of some insecticides.

Farmers today use twelve times the amount of pesticides than was used in 1945 and because of technology the increased productivity of farming has meant that 10 million acres of land are now redundant.

Fig 82. Burton Dassett Hills

Challenges to the Countryside, Agribusinesses, Fewer People Working the Land

After the War it became widely realised that agricultural land makes up most of the countryside and that more intensive agriculture was likely to be a threat to the landscape and public enjoyment of the land. The existing planning system was intended to protect the countryside from inappropriate urban growth but also it was necessary to rely greatly on help and goodwill from farmers to protect the landscape. Farming in this decade was made up of a great variety of businesses from the family dairy or pig farmer to large 'agribusinesses' aggressively growing cereals and producing meat. In some places this increased the variety of agricultural methods and crops grown with there was increased diversity in the landscape but in some areas there were large tracts of very similarly farmed land which meant far less variety.

Developments in technology, including more intensive farming, led to landscape changes through mechanisation, pollution and destruction of wildlife. For example herbicides caused a general reduction in many wild plants. It was soon estimated that so-called scientific farming had the potential to reduce the number of species of wildlife in the countryside by 80%.

149

The trend for fewer people to be employed in farming continued and this had an increasing effect on villages as unemployed agricultural workers left for jobs in the towns and city dwellers moved into their homes in the villages. The abandoned cottages were then done up for the city types and were far too expensive for the locals to live in. They changed in appearance, were tidied up and extended and in general became 'gentrified'. As village life declined the old school, the old forge and the old bakehouse closed and they were converted to homes. Very few villages were left with any means of production.

Increased leisure time began to lead to increased pressure on the countryside for recreation purposes such as walking and sports. Popular footpaths in areas such as national parks began to look tired and worn at the end of the decade. Building and other development was taking agricultural land at an increasing rate; 17,500 hectares per annum from 1945 to 1950.

The Rise of the Motor Car, New Towns,
New Town and Country Planning Regime

In 1948 public transport was still by far the most popular method of getting around and 60% of people travelled to work by rail or bus, many by bicycle with only 14% going by car. However there was a growing awareness of congestion and bottlenecks in villages and towns and roads such as the Coleshill by-pass were built soon after the war.

This was the decade when full-blown town and country planning was seen to be essential. 'Planning' as we will call it was really inspired by the need to supervise urban development which was in danger of running away into the countryside without effective control. From 1942, 73% of England was, in theory, subject to interim development control, but only 5% of the country was subject to operative schemes and this did not include Warwickshire. In 1944 regional plans had been developed for four regions but not in the West Midlands. Warwickshire was very vulnerable. Also in that year there were as many as 1,400 planning authorities in England with an out-dated system of local government.

It was decided that some overspill population from the major conurbations should be housed in new and expanded towns. In 1946 the Reith Report into New Towns was published and this led to the New Towns Act and set the stage for a number of new towns which were to be constructed by ad hoc development agencies over many years.

In the period 1945 to 1947 a Development Plan for Leamington Spa was drawn up by CH James and S Rowland Pierce but it was never implemented. The plan was intended to control haphazard growth to prevent the continuation of the pre-war tendency for towns to sprawl ever further into the countryside. The plan was for a five year programme of building of housing, schools and light industry. Alongside this the town's corporation was aiming for Leamington Spa to be an inland resort and conference centre as well as a spa. The corporation acquired 307 acres of land at Newbold Comyn Farm for a new hospital but it was never built and the site later became the present-day open space with a golf course and a swimming pool.

The first Act of Parliament referring to Town Planning dates from 1909 but the current legislation on the subject has its origins in the landmark Town and Country Planning Act 1947 that introduced the system that has been in use for over 60 years. The 1947 Act has been amended in its details and consolidated many times up to the present day. The Act was the first truly comprehensive attempt to control the development of all land. There were many strands of control most of which persisted in one form or another until the present time and are incorporated in the Town and Country Planning Act 1990. However the system is now gradually being redrafted under the Planning and Compulsory Purchase Act of 2004 which has introduced Local Development Frameworks.

The main provisions of the Town and Country Planning Act 1947 comprised a Carrot and Stick approach to the control of development. In effect development rights and development values were nationalised. Development plans were made mandatory and each of the remaining 145 local planning authorities (counties and county boroughs) were required to write a Plan within three years and to review it every five years.

The key requirement was that permission was required for most development and the first stage of that process was the submission of a planning application. There is a general rule that an application should be granted permission unless there is a good reason to refuse it. Agriculture was generally excluded from these planning controls on development. A subsidiary provision of the Act was that there was power for local authorities to control outdoor advertising. The Act also gave local authorities power to compulsorily purchase land to sell to private developers and to preserve woodland and buildings.

Homes for Heroes, Prefabs,
Growth of Industry

The government pledged in 1944 that there would be no more suburban dormitories and the prime minister, Clement Attlee, in 1945 promised to build 'Homes fit for heroes' for those who had returned from the War. From 1947 the pace of council house building grew rapidly and there was a licensing scheme to control private building because of the shortage of building materials. One innovation was that prefabricated houses were erected, to 11 approved designs, as part of the Temporary Housing Programme, between 1944 and 1948. This scheme was devised by the Burt Committee to relieve the post-war housing shortage at a time when conventional materials were not available. Almost 160,000 'prefabs' were built in the UK by 1948 at a cost of close to £216 million and there were 4,625 in Birmingham. They also appeared in Bedworth, Lillington and Whitnash. Prefabs at Wake Green Road, Birmingham are listed buildings. An example from Yardley is preserved at the Avoncroft Museum near Bromsgrove.

Fig 83. A Prefab from Yardley which is preserved at the Avoncroft Museum

In 1948 it was estimated that one-third of the houses in Birmingham needed replacement because they did not meet current quality standards. However in 1948 the report entitled 'Conurbation' contended that Birmingham did not need to expand to meet housing needs and the germ of the idea of the West Midlands Green Belt was born. Of course post war reconstruction in Warwickshire included the massive rebuilding of Coventry, destroyed in the Blitz.

This was a decade in which factories were run down because of a lack of maintenance while they were carrying out war work. There was also disruption of production as military personnel moved into civilian jobs. It was foreseen during the war that it was necessary to plan the location of industrial premises and the Distribution of Industry Act in 1945 signalled the start of regional planning. In Leamington in 1947 there was a plan for 210 acres of rural land to be used for light industry including 75 acres at Sydenham Farm but this was delayed because it needed a new road access to be built across the canal. At this time Coventry was primarily manufacturing cycles and cars which employed 10,000 people. The Spittalfields area in Bedworth was originally largely occupied by weavers and these old factories were eventually replaced by the Civic Hall.

National Parks, AONBs, Nature Conservancy

In this period, at the national level, the Conservative MP Duncan Sandys was very actively supporting a planned future for the countryside. Lord Sandys has been president of the Worcestershire branch of CPRE for many years. It was largely through his influence that the idea of conservation areas was incorporated in the law. This movement at this time was part of what has since been referred to as an 'Ecological Enlightenment'. From 1944 the national parks movement began to gather momentum based, amongst other influences, on the example of the National Park established at Cevennes in France. The government introduced the National Land Fund in 1946 and Chancellor Hugh Dalton said *"I should like to think that through the Fund we shall dedicate some of the loveliest parts of this land to those that died in order that we may live in freedom"*. The Dower report in 1945 made recommendations on the establishment of National Parks and this led to the National Parks & Access Act 1949. National Parks now cover as much as 25% of the land in England and Wales.

The Areas of Outstanding Natural Beauty were established under an Act of 1949 and now there are 35 of them in England. The Cotswolds AONB was designated in 1966 and includes areas in the far south and south west of Warwickshire. The landscape characteristics of the Cotswolds arise largely from the underlying strata of Jurassic limestone.

The Nature Conservancy Council, established under a charter of 1949, started to establish National Nature Reserves and Sites of Special Scientific Interest. Its functions were taken into English Nature in 1991. Country estates continued to be broken up because there was a high rate of taxation on inherited wealth. This meant that a number of parks such as at Shrubland House in Leamington, Haseley Old Manor, Oldbury Hall and Hall End Hall in Polesworth were lost.

Listed Buildings,
Footpaths, Trees

Building preservation orders were introduced in the Town and Country Planning Act 1932 but there was no systematic listing of buildings until after the new Act in 1947. This Act of 1947 created a regime of Listed Buildings and Scheduled Ancient Monuments and structured searches for suitable candidates for listing were conducted in the 1950s and 1960s. The current criteria for listing are that all buildings in anything like original condition from before 1700 are listed. Most worthy buildings from 1700 to 1840 are also listed. Buildings from 1840 to 1914 which have definite quality and character are listed, but only the best works of principal architects. From 1914 there is only a selection of high quality buildings listed. Buildings from all these categories are listed in Warwickshire and many are conspicuous features in the landscape. The most precious buildings are Grade I, the next are Grade II* and the next Grade II. Many of the Grade I and Grade II* buildings are churches and country houses and there are some more unusual constructions preserved such as a telephone kiosk at Shustoke, a dovecote at Kinwarton and some post war prefabs in Birmingham. See Appendix 4 for a list of a few of the listed buildings in Warwickshire arranged in districts and boroughs.

Protection for listed buildings is that any changes have to be requested by way of special planning permission and all applications are referred to English Heritage for an opinion. A local authority can issue a Certificate of Immunity from Listing. If a listed building is under threat then a local authority can compulsorily acquire it. A local authority can also issue a building preservation notice on unlisted building which lasts for six months but the local authority can be liable to pay compensation if the building is not listed eventually.

There are over 200 categories of sites which may be classified in another designation as scheduled ancient monuments. For example, there are 26 scheduled ancient monuments in north Warwickshire including a number of road bridges, Astley Castle, Oldbury Camp at Hartshill and Polesworth Abbey.

Under the National Parks and Access to the Countryside Act 1949 local authorities were able to negotiate access agreements to land for walkers. This procedure was mainly used in the Peak District at this time. Nowadays county councils maintain a definitive map of public paths. Long distance footpaths and National trails were also a post-war concept. The Town and Country Planning Act 1947 also introduced the power for local authorities to protect trees.

Chapter Eighteen

The 1950s

Cold War Defences, More People Lost from the Land, Hedgerows Uprooted

After the war a number of Cold War defence facilities were constructed. Most were in towns but notable sites in the countryside included the RAF V-bomber base at Gaydon, the nuclear bomb store at Lighthorne Rough, a headquarters building at Church Lawford, a bunker at Stoneleigh Deer Park and Charwelton BT tower (300 metres from Warwickshire boundary in Northamptonshire). There were also a number of underground monitoring posts and remains are still visible at Bidford-on-Avon, Barford, Wolston and Meriden. As already noted Bramcote airfield became a naval site named HMS Gamecock and then became an Army base (Gamecock Barracks) in 1959.

It has been estimated that in 1950 around 50% of the working population was still employed in connection with agriculture. However this percentage shrank quickly during the 1950s and the following decades. Farmers were still busy digging out hedges and trees so that they could make more efficient use of the land and therefore gradually spoiling what many regarded as the traditional appearance of the countryside and also the habitats of birds, animals and wild plants. In this decade a peak rate of 5,000 miles of hedgerows were being lost each year in England and Wales. The need for the government to support agriculture was recognised and ADAS, the Agricultural Development and Advisory Service, was established in 1957. It now operates as an arm's length agency.

Contaminated Land, Growth in Motor Cars, Decline in Public Transport

One of the problems with the policy of encouraging the re-use of brown-field land for development was that many of the old industrial sites were contaminated and therefore were very expensive to clean up before further use. The Environment Act 1955 was the first legislation to regulate this problem.

A phenomenon of this decade was that the number of motor cars nearly trebled from 1.8 million to 4.9 million and that the total number of all road vehicles more than doubled from 4.0 million to 8.5 million. The Buchanan Report on transport was published in 1958 and reached the not unsurprising conclusion that the motor car was a mixed blessing. On the one hand he acknowledged that it gave freedom to the owner of the car but it also created road congestion which was a hindrance and annoyance to others. This report signalled a period of intensive road-building and the M1 and the M45 link into Warwickshire were both opened in 1959.

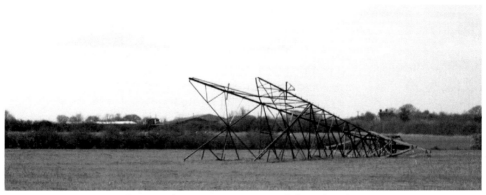

Fig 84. Pylon at Napton. Hopefully a sign that
electricity cables in the countryside will be buried underground in future

Accompanying this growth in personal mobility was the marked decline in the provision of public transport. In 1953 the tram services in Birmingham stopped and this was followed by the end of trolley buses in 1963. Many passenger railways were also closed including those from Leamington to Rugby in 1959, from Leamington to Weedon in 1958 and from Stratford to Blisworth in 1952. Kineton and Flecknoe stations closed to passengers in 1952 and Shilton closed in 1957. The age of the motor car had arrived with a vengeance. A worrying sign from experience in the USA was the growth of edge of town shopping centres alongside freeways. This trend led to out-of-town shopping centres in the UK in the following decades which gobbled up yet more green fields.

New Towns, Slum Clearance,
Planning Laws Expand

In the 1950s the building of eight new towns in a ring around London continued but no such high profile ventures were authorised in the Midlands. In their place the Town Development Act 1952 foresaw a series of overspill towns. Two of the Birmingham overspill towns were developed close to the

156

Warwickshire county boundary at Redditch and Daventry and a later one in the 1960s at Tamworth. Alongside urban growth and expansion slum clearance began again after the war and gathered momentum from 1955 onwards and was further encouraged by the 1957 Slum Clearance Act. This meant that more houses were built on green-field sites beyond the existing suburbs. The demand for housing also increased as the birth rate rose and there was increasing immigration, notably at this time from Ireland and the West Indies, and therefore private and council house building boomed. There was a continuing trend for young people to move to the towns leaving older people living in the countryside and the villages. To see things in perspective, it may be less than sixty years ago but it is surprising to recall that in 1950 there were many villages without a piped sewerage system.

In this decade the development of Manor Farm land in Lillington began in the Leamington Spa area and in the following year the Leamington Corporation gave loans to various developers for the provision of housing. At the same time land at Sydenham in the south-east of Leamington was purchased by a speculator and sold to a developer in 1959 who agreed to use the land to provide housing, industry, schools and allotments and open space.

For the first time since the war the Conservatives formed the government and they very soon abolished development or betterment charges and development rights were also extinguished. In 1959 the basis for the compensation for compulsory purchase of land and property became the fair market price. In this decade planning was not generally carried out thoroughly enough because of a shortage of professional planners. For example only three local plans had been approved by 1955 in the whole of the West Midlands under the 1947 planning regime.

Conservation, Green Belts,

In this decade the conflict between town and country was centre stage and, at last, a number of Green Belts were established around the country. Green Belts were a concept developed by Raymond Unwin at this time and were supported by the government minister, Duncan Sandys. There is little doubt that without the West Midlands Green Belt Birmingham and Coventry would now be joined together. The key purpose of establishing Green Belts was to prevent development on land between the conurbations but development for agriculture, forestry, sport, recreation, 'institutional use', golf courses, playing fields, horse riding, footpaths, major roads and other general development in exceptional circumstances was permitted.

Chapter Nineteen

The 1960s

Agricultural Chemicals Under Attack,
Dutch Elm Disease, Common Land

As the year 1960 came and went about 70% of the West Midlands region was still farming land but with fewer hedges and correspondingly larger fields than in the past. The vast majority of the farming land was being used intensively for raising crops but farming was so successful that there were surpluses of some crops. Criticism of the use of chemicals in farming came to the fore and there was a reduction in the use of the most insidious and persistent substances and the organochlorides, including Aldrin, Dieldrin and DDT, were totally banned.

In the late 1960s and onwards into the 1970s many views, particularly in the Feldon area of the county, were transformed as Dutch elm disease killed all the elm trees and they had to be felled. The disease is caused by fungi spread by elm bark beetles and it was first recorded in 1965 and appears to have originated in the vicinity of Tewkesbury.

In the late 1960s a more defined attempt at countryside planning emerged and a countryside forum, the Farming and Wildlife Advisory Group (FWAG), was established in 1969. A key planning event was that Lord Porchester obtained compensation for not being permitted to plough some of his land on Exmoor. The policy of the Forestry Commission for the widespread planting of conifers came under fierce attack for a number of reasons including evidence that oak woodland supports 284 different insects whereas a forest of firs supports only 16 of them.

There was a resurgence of interest in the future of common land at this time and the Commons Registration Act was passed in 1965. It was estimated that there were 400,000 hectares of common land remaining in England and Wales. Local authorities were required by the Act to keep a register of town and village greens as well as commons and a body of Commons Commissioners were appointed to settle disputes. These disputes arose because of the scarcity of written records and hearings had to be held to refer back to documents of enclosures, perhaps up to four hundred years old. Around 140 cases are recorded for Warwickshire ranging from Dordon in the north to Cherington in the south. If no owner is found then the land is registered as common land and has to be protected by the local authority. Ownership of land which is identified as a village green is often registered with the name of the parish council. As we have seen traditionally common land was used for such purposes as grazing of animals, gathering firewood and digging peat.

New towns, High rise housing,
Further Growth of Leamington

35,000 new homes were being built each year in the West Midlands region by the early 1960s. The Land Commission was established in 1967 to identify suitable building land but it only survived until 1971 when it was scrapped by the incoming Conservative government. The purpose of the Commission was to buy development land and the Commission soon identified shortages of land for new housing in the West Midlands.

In the years after the Act of 1946 the construction of 14 new towns was begun in the country and as we have seen the nearest to Warwickshire were at Redditch to the west, which became a new town in 1964, and Telford to the north and west designated in 1963. In 1964 the construction of huge estates of high-rise housing began at Chemsley Wood in the heart of the ancient Arden forest in Warwickshire after a public inquiry rejected alternative proposals for housing at Wythall just over the Warwickshire border in Worcestershire.

The construction of high-rise housing was very popular with the government despite the fact that the resulting population density was often little different from that achieved with conventional housing. However the disastrous consequences of the explosion at Ronan Point on 16th May 1968 signalled the virtual end of high-rise housing but the construction of high-rise offices continued. In the race to build houses there was no accepted standard for them from the end of the war to the start of this decade but from 1961 the Parker Morris standards began to be generally accepted and became mandatory for public housing in 1967. These standards were based on experience in the model town of New Earswick in Yorkshire which was developed by Joseph Rowntree beginning as long ago as 1902.

In this decade there was a discernible move of people from the towns back into the villages in the country. The Caravan Sites and Control of Development Act 1960 was passed to further control the use of land for caravans.

The 1960s was a time when Leamington Spa expanded further into its rural surroundings. In 1960 the county development plan identified open land at Sydenham Farm to the south east of the town for housing and industry and also Queensway as a trading estate beyond the boundary in the south west. Allotment land was bought to allow access to the Sydenham development along with the abandoned railway line to Rugby. Other land to the east running from

159

Holly Walk to Newbold Comyn was also acquired for housing as was land well to the south of the town at Golf Lane in Whitnash.

Fig 85. Daw Mill colliery in 2009 is the only working pit in the county

Daw Mill Colliery, Transport, The Rise of the Motor Car, Beeching Railway Closures

This was a time when many collieries in Warwickshire were closing as they became uneconomic. However Daw Mill colliery opened in 1965 to the north-west of Coventry. Initially Daw Mill was simply a ventilation shaft for the mine workings at Dexter Colliery but the shaft was later modified for coal winding. The first coal was brought up the shaft in 1965 and three years later a second shaft was added. In 1982 the decision to commission a surface drift was taken.

This decade was a time when motor road vehicles were considered in transport policy to require and deserve priority. Commuting by car rose by 14% in the five years from 1960 to 1965 and the use of buses fell by 25% in the same period. In 1965 60% of all trips were made by car. Pedestrians seemed to be regarded as a nuisance who deserved only to be buried in underpasses and subways.

From 1968 local authorities were required to develop a Transport Plan under the new Town and Country Planning Act. The policy on road building at this time was a 'predict and provide' principle based on the assumption that demand for roads was uncontrollable. It was calculated that 1 kilometre of motorway took 12.5 hectares of land (or 1 mile took 50 acres) and there was also a further land-take for motorway service areas such as that at Corley. The impact on Warwickshire peaked with the opening of the M5 and M6 in the middle of the decade. The Transport Act 1968 created the West Midlands Passenger Transport Authority which was set up in an attempt to provide an integrated passenger service throughout the region to challenge the use of the private car.

Fig 86. 'Mount Jud', the spoil heap from Judkins Quarry at Nuneaton

During the decade the report by Richard Beeching on the railways led to the closure of many branch lines including Ashchurch to Redditch (1963), Aylesbury to Rugby (the Great Central Line) (1966), Castle Bromwich to Walsall (1965), Honeybourne to Stratford (1969), Leamington Spa to Nuneaton (1965), Rugby to Leicester (1962), Rugby to Nottingham (1969) and Rugby to Peterborough (1966). Stations were also closed at Alcester (1963), Coleshill (1968), Fenny Compton (1964), Harbury (1964), Kineton (1965) and Long Marston (1966 & 1970).

Nature has soon reclaimed many of the abandoned lines and some have been converted to footpaths and cycle ways. The closures added to the enthusiasm for travel by car and road-building. On the other hand significant investment was made in some key railway routes such as the electrification of the West Coast Main Railway Line from Euston through Rugby, Coventry, Nuneaton and Atherstone and into Birmingham. Alongside these land-based developments air travel increased and in 1966 the main runway at Birmingham airport was extended.

Out of town shopping, Population, Green Belt, Cold War Constructions

Towards the end of the 1960s there was a move towards out-of-town hypermarkets which led to the loss of yet more countryside but this trend has since been largely reversed. In 1960 the population of West Midlands was reasonably well concentrated and 60% of the people lived in 5% of the area. From 1960 there were serious discussions throughout the West Midlands about establishing a green belt to surround Birmingham and other major urban areas which would be referred to in county development plans. In 1962 another Town and Country Planning Act formalised the designation of green belts.

A further unexpected reason for building in the countryside was the construction of an inconspicuous Nuclear Monitoring Post at Lawford Heath along with Emergency Government Bunkers in towns. Also erected at this time was the BT tower at Charwelton which is only 300 metres from Warwickshire and very visible from the county. Most of these towers are steel but this one was built of concrete on the recommendation of the Royal Fine Arts Commission and is 118 metres high. It is ironic that a metal lattice tower now stands alongside. The other BT towers which are nearest to Warwickshire are at Coalville and Stokenchurch.

Planning System, Conservation Areas

A Planning Advisory Group was set up in 1964 by the government and its advice led to the system of structure plans and local development plans which was set out in the 1968 Act. Although they were developed locally the regional structure plans had to be approved by the Minister. The new system was intended to harness the benefits which computers were expected to bring to the mapping and tracking of development. However work on plans was significantly disrupted by the reorganization of the structure of local government in 1974. The planning process moved from a 'prescriptive and definitive' process to one which was 'permissive and enabling' following the Skeffington Report in 1969; this also advocated a bottom up approach which was intended to use modern methods for achieving community involvement.

A West Midlands Regional Study in 1965 was set up by the Department of Economic Affairs and in 1969 there was a Coventry, Solihull and Warwickshire Sub-Regional Study managed from an office in Kenilworth. This continues in a different form today. Under the guidance of the government minister Duncan Sandys (yet again) the Civic Amenities Act 1967 introduced the concept of conservation areas and the ability for local authorities to further control development in those designated areas. In the next year the Countryside Act expanded on ideas for conserving the countryside by replacing the National Parks Commission with the Countryside Commission which was to set up regional and country parks.

Chapter Twenty

The 1970s

European Influences, A Decade of Change,

As the years go by it becomes more and more difficult to see what factors are really driving which changes in the countryside. One factor in this decade was that the European political dimension became important without a widespread realisation of the effects it would have in future years. At the same time a number of Government agencies were reformed and redesigned with new terms of reference and the powers of regional and local government were reassessed. Market forces also impacted on farming, industry, transport and housing growth.

All this altered the landscape to a significant extent. The apparently inexorable move to use agricultural land and other parts of the countryside for built development and other purposes continued. Between 1970 and 1975 the transfer of land from farming to development in Britain was about 12,000 hectares per year but this slowed a little at the end of the decade to 9,300 hectares per year - in other terms an area of countryside the size of Berkshire was being lost every 5 years. In 1976 there was a government circular which aimed to prevent this loss of agricultural land.

Industrialised Agriculture,
Agriculture and the Countryside, The EEC

Farming businesses calculated that ploughing up one mile of hedgerow produced about 2 more hectares (5 acres) of land for cultivation and between 1951 and 1975 over 80,000 kilometres (50,000 miles) of hedges were lost. This trend was also fuelled by the need to use increasingly large machines as efficiently as possible. There was also a move to plough up pasture to grow grain. Ironically this was a reversal of the enclosures when open fields were subdivided to graze and rear sheep. In 1972 only about 3,560 hectares (8,790 acres) of old woodland remained in England and there were only 56 surviving wood pastures. In 1973 Buchanan labelled many farmers as 'ruthless businessmen'.

Fig 87. Borage crop at Hill Wootton

In 1972 the Countryside Commission produced a report called 'New Agricultural Landscapes'. This led the way in trying to persuade politicians and farmers to have regard to the value of the countryside for purposes other than food production. There was also recognition of the need to retain as much biodiversity as possible so that the Nature Conservancy was set up in 1975 and the Conservation of Wild Creatures and Wild Plants Act was enacted. This was followed in 1978 by the Strutt Report on 'Agriculture and the Countryside' which was the first major report to recognise the emerging and ever more evident conflict between agriculture as an industry and the value of the countryside for people not involved in farming. The report called on interested parties to come together to find a mutually acceptable way forward.

Of course a major force for change in agriculture was the decision of Edward Heath's Conservative government to join the European Economic Community in 1973. The effects were soon felt from 1974 as price support of certain crops reduced diversity of cultivation and there was also a negative impact on environmental issues. One other thing we learnt from Europe was that one hectare equals 2.47 acres. Other forces were also in action as in the 1970s as a further 11million elm trees were lost to Dutch Elm Disease and Warwickshire said farewell to its last otters.

Out of Town Shopping, The NEC, Motorways,
The West Midlands Conurbation

The business of retailing changed significantly as out of town shopping became popular and Asda opened the first out of town supermarket nearby in Bloxwich at Walsall in 1971. The first full-blown out of town shopping centre was at Brent Cross in north London in 1976 and by the end of the decade there was an out of town centre shopping revolution. The main factors encouraging this trend were the availability of the motor car, the difficulty of parking in town centres and the relatively low cost of land out of town.

In the county in the early 1970s there was a highly controversial proposal for a major regional shopping centre at Stonebridge in Packington parish. The proposal was for 75,000 square metres of shopping space and 7,000 parking places which was equivalent to the whole of the shopping area in the centre of Coventry. This proposal went to a public inquiry in 1973 and there was a major stand-off between the owners of property on the Packington estate and the local authorities because the councils of Birmingham, Coventry, Solihull and Warwickshire all opposed the proposal. They were united in their concern about the threat to the existing city and town centres. The plan was eventually turned down. This decision on the Stonebridge proposal had a profound influence on the future of planning policy in the West Midlands. Following on from this the Midlands Branch of the Royal Town Planning Institute produced a report in 1977 entitled 'Predicting Shoppers' Requirements'.

A major development in the county which obtained consent in this decade was the National Exhibition Centre in the Green Belt near to Birmingham airport and the West Coast Main Line railway. The NEC is now 200,000 square metres with 20,000 parking spaces (three times the size of the shopping centre proposal at Stonebridge). At this time the Royal Show also became established at Stoneleigh Park in the Green Belt. Further north the biggest supermarket in the whole country at the time opened at Minworth in 1978. This was originally built by Carrefour and has since been taken over by Asda and it has recently received a major refurbishment after 30 years.

The decade saw a raft of major new roads in the county. In 1972 the Midland Links motorways including the M5 and M6 were finished with the iconic Spaghetti Junction and Corley service area. In the 1970s proposals for the construction of the M40 and M42 were approved after enduring prolonged public inquiries and plans were also made for the Warwick and Kenilworth by-pass (A46). However in 1972 a government report advocated a national policy to promote public transport and the 'balanced approach' to getting around. This is now called the 'sustainable solution' and it has taken many years for policy-makers to catch on.

The confusion in planning policy at this time is illustrated by a number of emerging structure plans and other plans for the region. In 1973 the Birmingham Structure Plan aimed to increase development around train stations and the Coventry Structure Plan provided for only 70% of journeys being made by car and required parking restraint and also better public transport. On the other hand the Solihull Structure Plan in 1972 aimed to provide for all the demands for roads on the 'predict and provide' principle. A White paper entitled 'Putting People First' in 1972 led to increased compensation for the distress caused to people by new roads and national policy began to look more critically at the need for roads. In 1977 a Trunk Road Assessment was introduced, in 1984 there was the Urban Road Appraisal, in 1992 the Assessment of Environmental Impact and finally in 1994 the question was asked 'Do New Roads Generate Traffic?'.

Fig 88. The edge of Berkswell - where modern housing meets the countryside

The Sydenham Estate, Housing Policy,
Local Government Reorganisation

In Leamington Spa the Sydenham industrial state was already well developed and a new bridge at the end of Prospect Road was built over the railway to give access to the new estate from the west. Stanleys Lane became known as Sydenham Drive and gave access from the Radford Road across a new bridge over the canal. The Sydenham estate spread over an area of 100 hectares (250 acres) with 1500 houses and 50 acres of industrial development.

In this decade the wholesale clearance of unsuitable houses was replaced by a policy of housing improvement. In 1977 the programme for the construction of new towns was discontinued and the New Towns Corporation was wound up. However Tamworth was identified as a site for the continuing policy of providing overspill from Birmingham. Policy on high rise dwellings was also reviewed and the lack of gardens was identified as an important shortcoming. The training ground for Aston Villa football club was established at Bodymoor Heath in the north of the county.

The Royal Commission on Local Government, chaired by Lord Redcliffe-Maud, sat from 1966 to 1969 and recommended how reorganisation of local government should take place. The proposals included the merging of Warwickshire with Coventry and the addition of a few parishes in Northamptonshire to the county. The legislation in 1972, which came into force in 1974, of course, kept the county and Coventry separate and also left alone the targeted parishes in Northamptonshire. The West Midlands County Council was formed with seven Metropolitan Districts including Coventry and Solihull. Solihull was extended into Warwickshire to include Chelmsley Wood and the Meriden Gap and Birmingham absorbed Sutton Coldfield from the county. Five district councils or boroughs of North Warwickshire, Nuneaton and Bedworth, Rugby, Warwick and Stratford-on-Avon were established in the new administrative county of Warwickshire.

National Turmoil,
Countryside Policy as a Political Football, Green Belt

The 1970s were a time of political turmoil. The Conservative government had to deal with Rolls Royce being declared bankrupt, postal workers on strike for a 19.5% pay increase and the miners on strike. A state of emergency was declared in 1972 and 1973. The miners were given a 35% pay rise in 1974 and the recession in the 1970s led to high unemployment which was up to 1.25 million. There was a three day week in 1974, public expenditure was cut and a 50 mph speed limit was introduced because of the oil shortage. During the Wilson government inflation reached 25% in July 1975 despite the 'social contract' in 1974. Finally there was the winter of discontent in 1978/9.

This was a decade when policy affecting the countryside kept wavering in direction. From 1970 to 1974 there was a Conservative government but in the second half of the decade there was a Labour government which was followed by the Conservatives again in 1979. It can be seen that in the 1970s land use planning became a political football along with many other policy areas.

Yet another attempt at reaping benefits for society from the granting of planning permission was made when in 1971 a development gains tax was introduced by the Conservatives together with a first letting tax on shops, offices and other businesses. There was also a proposed action against land hoarding in a Conservative White Paper.

This was followed by a community land scheme and the development land tax by Labour between 1974 and 1979. Labour introduced the Community Land Act in 1975 and the Development Land Tax in 1976. The Labour White Paper in 1977 entitled 'Policy for the Inner Cities' identified the problems with decaying economic and social conditions in many cities and proposed solutions to regenerate them and Coventry was one of the first cities to be identified for action. In 1979 the Conservatives regained power under Margaret Thatcher and a policy review was undertaken and details of this are in the next chapter.

When the Conservatives came to power in the 1970s the government began to use regulations to amend Acts of parliament and there was less scrutiny of new planning legislation by parliament. It has subsequently become more difficult to keep track of changes in planning legislation.

In 1975 the West Midlands Green Belt was finally approved by the Minister fourteen years after it was first proposed but 25% of the land was deemed to be only 'interim' Green Belt, a kind of second rate designation.

At a West Midlands Conference in 1976 there was more emphasis on renewing urban housing, predictions of population growth were significantly reduced and the social and economic problems in inner cities were recognised. A study entitled 'A Developing Strategy for the West Midlands' was published in 1971 and was revised in 1974.

Cow Green Reservoir, Amberley Wild Brooks, Conservation Areas, the Polluter Pays

A great deal of future planning policy is determined in test cases. A major milestone for conservationists was the symbolic fight to prevent the construction of Cow Green Reservoir in County Durham from 1969-1971. This campaign overall was unsuccessful but conditions were imposed that only 10% of the existing flora and fauna were to be destroyed. There was also the planning inquiry concerning Amberley Wild Brooks wetland area in West Sussex in 1975 which considered the conflict between the desirability of improving drainage and the conservation of wetland and on this occasion conservationists won the day. These two decisions had a profound effect on all councils and planning officers, including those in Warwickshire.

Various initiatives in Europe had a number of profound effects on planning policy in Britain. For example in 1970 the European Year of Conservation led to an increase in the conservation of buildings and areas and the European

Architectural Heritage Year in 1975 was an impetus for the listing of buildings. In 1972 control on demolition of buildings in conservation areas was introduced.

The 'Polluter Pays Principle' on pollution was formulated in 1975. This principle states that the person or company which causes pollution of the countryside, water or air quality should pay for cleaning up the pollution and other consequences.

Miscellany

The Woodland Trust was founded 1972 to protect ancient woods, improve woodland biodiversity, increase native woodland cover and increase understanding and enjoyment of woods. The Trust has woods at Great Alne, Corley Moor, Temple Balsall, Gibbet Hill, Kineton and Ilmington.

In the 1970s it was decided to create Kingsbury Water Park on the site of gravel workings in the north of Warwickshire and this is run by the county council. Following the post war surge in the number of visitors to the countryside in Britain levelled off during the 1970s.

Chapter Twenty-One

The 1980s

**Pressure on the Countryside, Nature in Crisis,
Agricultural Over-Production**

In this decade the increase in population and further economic growth continued to put pressure on the countryside and 5,000 hectares each year was transferred from agricultural use to urban use in England during the 1980s. There was also a loss of hedgerows of about 4,500 miles each year in the decade. From 1950 to 1985 it was reckoned that England lost 95% of its herb-rich meadows and 25% of hedgerows had gone together with 50% of lowland heaths. There was also widespread concern about the effects of the drainage of the land on wildlife because drainage leads to desiccation of the landscape and loss of wet habitats which are essential for some species. This varies over time with different drainage patterns, soil type, the weather and existing vegetation. The mechanisation of farming continued and the employment of contractors with their expensive machines became more common. All this change meant that 80% of the land surface of Britain was farmed by only 2.5% of workforce.

In 1953 there were 454,000 farms in England and Wales but by 1981 this had fallen to 242,300 (a reduction of 46%) mainly due to mergers of farms and the renting of fields to other farms. Many farmhouses therefore became private houses with no connection with the farming of the surrounding land.

In 1984 Britain produced 26 million tonnes of cereals which was a staggering 10 million tonnes more than we could eat. This meant that in effect 2.5 million acres of land was no longer required for agriculture because of EU surpluses. A major review was required and the concept of 'set-aside' was introduced in 1989 to implement EEC regulations. Under this scheme the government made payments to farmers who undertook to withdraw at least 20 per cent of the area of their land from agricultural production for a period of five years. Set-aside land had to be left fallow or used for woodland or for non-agricultural purposes. In addition, farmers entering the scheme had to restrict the growing of arable crops during the set-aside period. This had a dramatic impact on the appearance of the landscape because many fields were left uncultivated or were not being grazed by animals. This also led to more wildflower meadows and an increase in habitats for wildlife.

Fig 89. Corley Services on the M6

Conservation Again, Elm Disease

The Wildlife and Countryside Act of 1981 was an interesting innovation because it gave compensation to farmers for NOT developing a sensitive site. The Agriculture Act of 1986 was also encouraging because it aimed to improve the balance between the needs of agriculture and the wider rural, social and environmental interests. The Farm Woodland Premium Scheme was introduced in 1988 to encourage farmers to convert productive agricultural land to woodland by providing annual incentives in the form of payments for 10 years (for mainly conifer woodlands) or 15 years (for mainly broadleaved woodlands) to compensate for lost farming income.

Some elm trees were re-established after the Dutch elm disease disaster but virtually all of them finally succumbed to the disease in the 1980s and 1990s. The vast majority of 30 million elm trees had been killed in England. The elm bark beetle disappears as its habitat is killed but reappears quite quickly to infest new-grown trees. It is hoped that elms with immunity to the disease can be bred and scientists are trying to propagate from the very few mature trees that have survived.

The national organisation, the Small Woods Association, was established in 1988 to conserve, plant, manage or harvest woods and trees. People manage small woods for a wide range of benefits, to harvest timber, to support

172

woodland crafts, to encourage and enjoy the wildlife, or just for recreation. The importance of hedgerows is difficult to overstate, it is estimated that 10 million birds breed in 600,000 miles of hedgerows in England. Between 1947 and 1987 it has been estimated that 22% of hedgerows vanished in England and Wales. Research by the Countryside Commission shows that hedgerow trees made up 38% of all horizon views in Warwickshire but in 1987 this had reduced to only 4%. It is also estimated that the number of broad leaved trees in the landscapes of the West Midlands fell by a third between 1947 and 1982.

In every decade of the twentieth century it has been ironic that enthusiasts destroy what they covet by digging up rare plants or collecting eggs or killing and stuffing birds and animals.

Fig 90. A view from the tower of St Mary's Church in
Warwick looking over the Castle Park

Industrial Decline

By the 1980s coal mining in the county had declined and most pits had been closed. There was then a concentration of attention on the reclamation of colliery sites, slag-heaps, railway sidings and adjoining land for redevelopment. They are regarded by planners as previously developed sites but the choice of a new use is often difficult because they are adjacent to or in the midst of the countryside. Many colliery sites in the county, such as Birch Coppice, have been used for warehousing or industrial and business estates. The 'greening' of abandoned quarries also became a priority. The planning application for a new super-pit to produce coal at Hawkhurst Moor in the Green Belt to the west of Coventry in 1987 was refused.

The decline in manufacturing industry in Britain continued and factory sites were abandoned and debate began on what to re-use them for. Fortunately there was a growth in the demand for service industries to provide employment.

From 1980 there was a move towards mixed residential and business use of land with some businesses being permitted in residential or rural areas. In the 1980s the emphasis in the West Midlands was on investment in town and city centres in preference to out of town sites. However in 1985 and 1988 national planning policy guidance favoured out of town retailing unless the proposal was likely to damage an existing town or city shopping centre as a whole. The result was an uneasy balance between town centre shopping and out of centre retail development. In 1986 in Warwickshire there were about 21 large food stores in town centres and 10 out of town stores.

In the Leamington area in 1980 10 acres of green-field land at Heathcote to the south of the town were released for industry and a further 6 acres in that area were released in 1984. In addition in 1986 132 acres at Tachbrook Park was allocated for industry and in 1989 the Campion Hills allotments were sold for housing.

Giant Lorries, Public Transport

The sizes if commercial vehicles continued to increase and there were serious concerns about whether roads and, in particular, bridges could cope with the extra loads and the increased wear and tear. This increased the political pressure for new roads to provide alternatives for the old ones. The M42 from the M5 to the A38 (Bromsgrove to Shirley) was held up by protesters for 10 years but it eventually opened in phases. The Solihull section opened in 1976, the Umberslade section in 1985 and the section from Lickey End to Alvechurch in 1986. However the northern turn of the junction to the M5 at the Bromsgrove end did not open until 1989. The M69 from Coventry to the M1 opened throughout in 1977.

A White Paper on buses was published in 1984 and this led to an Act in 1985 which introduced deregulation by removing the complex system of licensing and this was followed by unrestricted competition. This has been a mixed blessing as some services have been lost and there was absurd competition on other routes, particularly in some towns and cities. There have also been cases of predatory services which run below cost to drive out competition.

Fig 91. The BT telecommunications tower at Charwelton, a few yards
from the Warwickshire boundary

Affordable Homes, Planning Policy Evolves

A major advance was the requirement for applicants for significant amounts of housing to provide a proportion of affordable homes on the site. The affordable homes are normally rented or held on a joint ownership basis under the control of a housing association.

Starting in 1964 15,000 homes, including 34 tower blocks, were built as Castle Vale in Chelmsley Wood in the Green Belt. The National Exhibition Centre and the expansion of Birmingham Airport also took place in the Green Belt. Following a public inquiry in 1979 the new main terminal at Birmingham

Airport was opened to handle 3 million passengers per year in 1984. In 1987 ownership of the airport transferred from the city council to a private company.

As noted in the previous chapter the Conservative government took power in 1979 and reviewed planning policy. They decided that there was to be less emphasis on planning and reduced concern for the environment and control on developers was loosened. The chase was on for economic performance and the power of market forces was paramount. All betterment taxes were abandoned. The Local Government Planning Act in 1980 removed the duty of development control from the county councils. The district councils which took over were generally more inclined to permit out of town shopping. The Act also diverted resources from the regions to the inner cities. The key White Paper in 1985 was entitled 'Lifting the Burden'. The changes in law which followed generally reduced planning controls yet further. Prime Minister Margaret Thatcher showed no concern for the environment until a key speech in 1988 at the party conference and from that moment policy changed yet again and the Conservative government warmly embraced the environment and its benefits.

The priorities for government spending are shown by the fact that only £10 million was spent on the Nature Conservancy Council and £2 million on the Countryside Commission but £5,000 million was allocated to agricultural support. The National Heritage Act of 1983 consolidated the law on ancient monuments and established English Heritage and the Agriculture Act in 1986 established the system of Environmentally Sensitive Areas. Across the Channel the European Union introduced regulations on emission standards. During this period the compulsory purchase powers of local authorities were strengthened.

Further influential events occurred outside Warwickshire which set important precedents across the country. For example in 1981 the demolition of the iconic Firestone factory, which was built in 1928 on the Great West Road in Brentford, led the impetus for the listing of important buildings. It is notable that the comparable Hoover building, also in west London, from the same period, has survived and now thrives under the protection of Tesco.

There is less restrictive planning control on the building and modification of farm buildings but notice has to be given to the planning authority and steps can be taken to prevent over-large or buildings of inappropriate appearance, especially in the Green Belt. People have objected to giant silos in the countryside which have an incongruous industrial appearance.

Prince Charles spoke out on planning matters with his famous 'carbuncle' speech about the proposed National Gallery extension in 1984 and he set out his ten priorities for good planning which were Place, Hierarchy, Scale, Harmony, Enclosure, Materials, Decoration, Art, Signs and Lights and Community.

Enterprise Zones were introduced by the government and in 1981 and 1984 zones in the West Midlands such as Merry Hill at Dudley were designated. At a similar time the Urban Development Corporations were established. The Black Country Development Corporation was set up in 1987 and the Corporation tackled derelict land areas in the 1980s and 1990s to enable them to be brought back into use. This recycling of land is essential to reduce demand for the development of previously undeveloped land in the countryside.

Two meadows of surviving ridge and furrow at Draycote were designated as Grade 2 conservation sites by the Nature Conservancy in the early 1980s.

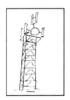

Chapter Twenty-Two

The 1990s

Government Changes, Climate Change,

This was a decade in which changes in the political colour of the British government and global concern about climate change both had profound impacts on thinking about the environment. There was much debate about whether climate change, or global warming, was actually happening and whether the acts of mankind were causing the changes. There was also an avalanche of government edicts of one sort or another affecting land-use planning.

Fig 92. Harvest Time. Hay ricks have evolved into all shapes of bales

178

Agribusinesses, Stewardship Schemes,
McSharry Reforms, GMOs

Over the period of years since the war there was a move from the use of the term 'Agriculture' to the rather more aggressive word 'Agribusiness' which was largely caused by the urge for the country to become self sufficient in food production. In consequence the proportion of land in the hands of entrepreneurial farmers and landowners was increasing quickly. As we saw in the previous chapter the total number of farms had halved. At the beginning of this decade there was rising concern about the impact that these and other changes in agriculture were having on the countryside.

The Countryside Stewardship Scheme (CSS) run by the Countryside Commission and funded by the government was introduced in 1991. This included countryside grant programmes and a countryside premium together with woodland grants and other special schemes for environmentally sensitive areas. One such scheme which was grant-aided was at Ditchford Farm at Shipston-on-Stour where rare bumblebees had been discovered.

Some of the planting of areas on the University of Warwick site on the Coventry border has also been funded by the CSS. The CSS, which operated in Warwickshire from 1996 until 2004, has also supported the creation of 23 hectares of conservation headland where fertiliser was used, 53 hectares of conservation headland where fertiliser was not used and 1068 kilometres of 6 metre arable field margins. CSS has been succeeded by the Environmental Stewardship Scheme which continues into 2009. Good farming practice, including care of field margins, beetle banks and conservation headlands can be seen on many farms in the county where the farmer has an interest in demonstrating the farm's environmental credentials.

Meanwhile in Europe the McSharry reforms of the European Common Agricultural Policy in 1992 encouraged environmentally friendly practices by introducing payments for farmers who pursued such policies. Other 'McSharry Reforms' helped to stabilise agriculture throughout the European community and went a long way to replacing the system of guaranteed prices with a new system of direct payments of compensation to farmers if prices fell below a certain level.

Evidence that a major feature of the landscape was disappearing was noted in 1991 when it was recorded that there were only 400,000 hectares of ancient woodland remaining in the whole of England and Wales which accounted for barely 2.6% of the land surface. The proportion in Warwickshire was slightly higher at around 4%.

Also of concern were the newly introduced methods of hedge cutting which were highly mechanised and there was concern that cutting by flail instead of saws or blades was demolishing the trees in the hedgerows. The timing of hedge cutting and the shape of the hedgerows has a dramatic effect on the appearance of the countryside. In this decade a once familiar blot on the autumnal landscape vanished when stubble burning was banned in 1993 because of atmospheric pollution and the damage it caused to adjoining hedges, trees and wildlife.

Technology continued to have a significant impact on agriculture and there was concern about the application of knowledge about genetics. Highly public controversy began to emerge about so-called genetically modified organisms (GMOs) such as maize and tomatoes which were widely cultivated in the USA but only grown to a very limited extent in Britain.

Fig 93. Alvecote Marina demonstrates the growth in the leisure use of canals

Hams Hall, Green Belt Threat,
Transport Policy, Birmingham Airport

A familiar blot on the North Warwickshire landscape started to disappear in this decade when the huge Hams Hall power station complex near Coleshill finally closed down in 1992. The first power station was opened on the site in the 1920s and before the power station was built the land was part of a large and peaceful country estate.

At its peak Hams Hall was one of the largest electricity generating stations in Europe with three generators and thirteen cooling towers. The site has not been returned to parkland but has quickly been covered by a large business park and railway interchange depot, the Channel Tunnel Freight Terminal.

The pressure for development in the Green Belt around Solihull was given high level scrutiny when there was a public inquiry in 1991 into as many as seven proposals for business parks around the M42. The outcome was the approval of just one site at the Blythe Valley Business Park in the Green Belt near Hockley Heath which covers 170 acres.

There was widespread speculation at this time that with the growth of computers there would be more people running businesses from home and there would be computing centres set up in the countryside close to where people lived. Further details of this development are in the next chapter.

In 1994 there was another national review of policy on the building of trunk roads and many previously proposed schemes were shelved. It was decided to improve the existing routes, build by-passes and reduce the amount of new trunk routes. In general the schemes with negative environmental effects were dropped and it was decided to build roads in the Green Belt only in the most exceptional cases. Alternatives to the motor car continued to be considered and in 1991 there were 40 proposals for rapid transport systems for conurbations in Britain on the drawing board. The Metro light rapid rail system in Birmingham was first envisaged in 1969 and eventually opened in 1999. Bus services were also encouraged by subsiding little used services from the surpluses on those which were well used. Alongside this a strategy for encouraging cycling was also being developed in 1996.

The seemingly inexorable development of Birmingham Airport continued with the opening of the second terminal, known as the Eurohub, in 1991. In 1996 the airport handled six million passengers and this soon increased, a mere three years later, to seven million.

Sustainability, Planning Policies, Footpaths, Endangered Plants

In 1995 a major area of allotments at Whitnash to the south of Leamington Spa was sold for housing after a long legal struggle and the main road into the site was named after a local policeman, PC Dobson. In 1998, 290 houses were built adjacent to the main Sydenham development to the south east of Leamington Spa. One aspect of national housing policy was changed to allow the building of iconic single large high quality houses in the countryside of an exceptional architectural design and a 'Georgian' hall of this type was built at Halford in 1990.

Once again in this chapter it is necessary to consider the cumulative effect of national laws and planning guidance on local development. The main 'political' concerns in this period were sustainability, the countryside, the environment, heritage sites, the use of redundant buildings, the use of the Green Belt, affordable housing and the plan-led system of development. There was much tinkering with the system and policies as the political parties again alternated in control of the government.

The new Holy Grail of 'Sustainability' became a major preoccupation in the 1990s. The concerns about sustainability were taken up in the Conservative White Paper on the Environment 'This Common Inheritance' which was published in 1990. There are many different opinions on what 'sustain' and 'sustainability' mean. In the purest sense as described in dictionaries it means to prolong or withstand without significant change. In 1994 a UK strategy emerged to ensure 'sustainability' in the rather more extensive sense that it meant an ethical approach to the development of the economy and the environment and required planning to take account of this. Sustainability was defined in the Town and Country Planning Act in 1992 and became embedded in planning policies. The four aims of sustainable development were refined in 1999 and are referenced in Policy Planning Statement No 1 as –

1. social progress which recognises the needs of everyone;
2. effective protection of the environment;
3. prudent use of natural resources; and,
4. maintenance of high and stable levels of economic growth and employment.

In 1992 representatives from nearly 180 countries met at the 'Earth Summit' in Rio de Janeiro to discuss how to achieve worldwide sustainable development. They agreed and published the Rio Declaration on Environment and Development which sets out 27 principles supporting sustainable development. An action plan, Agenda 21, was agreed and it was recommended that all countries should produce national sustainable development strategies.

Locally this led to the emergence of the organisation called 'Action 21' which supports greener, sustainable living in Warwickshire.

In 1991 the government encouraged the positive use of redundant buildings, such as hospitals, in the Green Belt. This led to developments at Weston-under-Wetherley and Hatton Park in the south of the county. There was also a government circular encouraging the construction of more affordable housing in 1991. The Conservative government published three White Papers relating to the countryside in 1995 and 1996 and they also published a consultation paper on protecting our heritage in 1996. However planning guidance in 1995 reaffirmed that some sites in the Green Belt could be developed in exceptional cases.

Fig 94. The River Avon in flood at Sherbourne may be symbol for climate change

The Planning and Compensation Act 1991 and the Town and Country Planning Act in 1990 reiterated the necessity for the 'plan-led system' which was established in 1947. Development Plans were seen as the key to controlling local development and the over-arching strategic Structure Plans were to be approved by county councils. At an administrative level the Planning Inspectorate (PINS) was established as an executive agency in 1992.

The review of local plans in the districts and boroughs became bogged down because the public inquiries into the plans were taking 50 weeks in 1995 whereas they took only about 7 weeks in 1988.

Other legislation has also had an influence on the county. The Wildlife Enhancement Scheme was established by English Nature in 1991 as a move to be more proactive and positive in managing the countryside. The Urban Regeneration Agency, also known as English Partnerships, was formed in 1999 to recover vacant urban land for development and hence spare some of the green fields. As an alternative to recouping planning gains from developers a scheme of Planning Obligations was set out in section 106 of the Town and Country Planning Act 1990. This specified that developers had to agree with councils to pay to provide the infrastructure which was required to support their development when it had been approved. The Environment Agency took over the National Rivers Authority, inspectors of pollution and the local authority waste regulation departments in 1996. In the world of planning

183

policies local authorities were urged to protect high grade agricultural land from development.

A growing threat to the environment at this time was that 400 million tonnes of waste were produced in England in 1990 (5% from households) and had to be disposed of somehow. This issue was turning into a time-bomb threatening the environment. Concern has led to the move to recycling and reduction of waste generation. The huge mountain of waste at Packington continued to be constructed.

In 1991 as many as 80% of the population of England and Wales lived in an urban environment. The sub-region of Coventry, Solihull and Warwickshire had seen a population increase of 40% from 1.0 million in 1967 to 1.4 million in 1991.

There were 5,700 Sites of Special Scientific Interest (SSSIs) designated in England and Wales by 1991. There are now 62 SSSIs in Warwickshire. The government claimed that 95 square kilometres of derelict land in the UK had been reclaimed in the period 1988 to 1993 from a total of 405 square kilometres. About 6% of Warwickshire is previously developed land of one sort or another. See the next chapter for more details.

The mobile phone industry began to take off in this decade and the blight of a closely knit pattern of mobile phone masts soon became an issue as important as the tall, striding lines of electricity pylons had been in the past. The phone masts tend to be grouped around main roads and junctions and each of the three or four networks has its own pattern of masts instead of sharing them. Sharing would be less intrusive in the landscape and this is encouraged by national planning policies. There was also concern about the possible impact of radiation from mobile phones on health but this was deemed not to be a planning matter.

The popularity of walking in the countryside gradually increased and Warwickshire county council has the duty to maintain the official maps of paths and there are over 2,730 kilometres (1,700 miles) of recognised public footpaths and bridleways in the county as well as many hundreds of miles of quiet roads and canal towpaths. The 'Right to Roam' was widely debated in this decade by proponents and opponents and was encapsulated in the Countryside and Rights of Way Act 2000. However no land in Warwickshire has been designated under this Act.

In 1992 the first British Red Data Book on scarce and endangered plants was issued. Fifteen endangered plants are being researched in Warwickshire in 2008 including the blue pimpernel, corn buttercup, corn gromwell, corn marigold, corn spurrey, dwarf spurge, field woundwort, large hemp-nettle, narrow-leaved hemp-nettle, night-scented catchfly, prickly poppy, shepherd's needle, spreading hedge-parsley, stinking chamomile and wild pansy.

Chapter Twenty-Three

The New Millennium:
The Twenty-first Century

Challenges Ahead,
Farming Futures - Production or Stewardship, Invasive Plants

Readers of this book who have got this far have travelled through many thousands of years to reach the present day. This chapter will now review the present state of the landscapes of Warwickshire, the threats and challenges which they face and the steps which may or should be taken to protect, improve, preserve or conserve the treasures which are left for us today.

Fig 95. The encouraging sight of a newly-planted hedge at Offchurch

Agriculture is obviously still the predominant land use but it is necessary to reassess where its values lie. It is necessary to review the different aspects of its contribution to society. Its value to the economy and its value as an employer have diminished. But perhaps its importance socially and culturally is growing in significance. A cynic may say that agricultural land is most valuable as land on which to build houses and businesses; after all this is usually more remunerative than conventional agriculture. There needs to be a fair and proper balance between these views but perhaps the most important thing to remember is that once agricultural (or any other undeveloped) land is lost it is very, very rarely regained.

We have seen that agriculture has had a major impact on the landscape of Warwickshire at every period from the Iron Age. The farming methods and settlements which grew from the time that agriculture became commonplace provide much of what many of us find most attractive about the landscapes of the county today. This will change in the first century of the third millennium. Eating habits of the population are changing quickly. The enthusiasm to become self-sufficient in food after 1945 has faded away and many people no longer wish to tolerate their diet being dictated by the changing seasons. Most fruits and vegetables are available at almost any time of the year, often from a farm on a distant continent. There is now the growth of some resistance to this as figures are published to identify the 'food miles' associated with imported produce and the possible impact on climate change. There is also an enthusiasm for organic food which is produced without the use of artificial fertilisers, pesticides and herbicides.

In 2002 the Habitat Biodiversity Audit identified 57,000ha of land under cereal crops and a total of 77,000ha of arable fields in Warwickshire. In addition there are smaller units of arable land such as allotments, smallholdings, parks and larger gardens. However, not all this area is suitable for the selected species of crops. For example, light sandy soils, which are favoured by some of the arable plants, are mostly found between Rugby and Grandborough, up to the county border to the east, the A423 Southam to Coventry road to the west and the Blythe and Tame valleys north of Meriden.

The Countryside Survey is published every ten years and is a comprehensive audit of long term changes to habitats and landscape features in the UK since 1978. The report in 2007 showed that most features are showing a serious decline in the decade since 1998. The length of managed hedgerows has reduced by 6.9%, the biological condition of ponds has declined and the quality of areas recognised for their botanical interest has also diminished.

The richness of arable plant species has increased by 30%, but much of this gain has since been put at risk by an expansion of cultivation after the phasing out of set aside and the rise in farm commodity prices.

As more varieties of food are imported from countries where production costs (or pay rates) are very low it has often soon become uneconomic to

186

produce food of that type in this country. Exacerbating this problem is the power of the increasing monopolies of the supermarkets which are forcing prices paid to farmers in Britain down to an uneconomic level.

Fig 96. Linseed near Ilmington is an example of the
diverse range of crops which is now grown

An important factor is a welcome change in the agricultural policy of the European Union. Funds are no longer given to farmers purely to subsidise food production but are paid on the basis of them maintaining and improving the environment. In many ways this appears to be beneficial but it is likely to lead to changes in the landscape. It is becoming increasingly unusual to see domesticated animals in the landscape and fields often have no identifiable growing crop. It is now becoming economic for farmers to just take the grants and leave the fields largely untouched for it remains difficult to fit conservation into a busy farm even when there are financial incentives.

It is notable that nowadays most farms specialise in a limited number of crops and have become easier to work and more efficient. This is in contrast to earlier practice where farms were much more diverse having orchards, paddocks, barns, coverts, ricks, dykes and coppices. There is consequently less marginal land such as hedges, ditches, corner spinneys, streams and steep banks.

187

There are many options for the future of farming which have to take into account at least eight factors including the general reduction in government support, targeting support on efficient farmers, encouraging less intensive farming, funding of set-aside, encouraging part time farming, encouraging diversification, more afforestation and conservation.

Countryside stewardship schemes have encouraged many farmers to think about conservation of wildlife and the countryside and to allow additional access to their land with permissive footpaths. Gradually this less intensive use of farming land has led to increase in wildlife, including an increase in the diversity of both animals and plants.

It will be necessary to decide how far our society wants the pendulum to swing away from use of the land for agriculture. Much of our enjoyment of the landscape comes from seeing the changing patchwork of fields as the texture and colour of the crops vary throughout the seasons and the changing views as cattle and sheep move in the fields and spend winter in barns. As we have seen this balance between natural and unnatural use of land requires a balance which historically has largely occurred by accident in response to external factors. The major deliberate use of land to improve views in the past has been the landscaping of large estates and their use for hunting.

As with many things in life we need to face up to the downsides of farming. Buildings such as tower silos and steel and asbestos barns can be unsightly even when they are essential for farming and especially if they are isolated and separate from other groups of buildings on the land. Uprooted hedgerows, ploughed up moorland and the burning of stubble are examples of problems in the past. 95% of lowland meadows have been destroyed. For good reasons there is also negative public reaction to the use of pesticides, factory farming and genetic engineering. GMO trials of disease resistant potatoes have recently taken place in East Yorkshire and Cambridgeshire but there have been none in Warwickshire since 2002.

Other landowners who do not farm their land also have a major impact on the countryside. For example, the management of woodland is important to the landscape. 90% of woodland is derelict coppice and can look worthless and unattractive and it can also be unprofitable. It must be noted that currently most changes to husbandry and management of land do not require planning permission. Hedgerows have been reduced by 80% since 1850. Heath plants such as gorse have taken root on slag heaps at abandoned mines.

Warwickshire Wildlife Trust looks after 50 reserves ranging from Alvecote in the north of the county to Tysoe Island in the south; 15 of these are Sites of Special Scientific Interest. There are still herds of deer at Charlecote Park, Packington Park and Sutton Park.

A threat which has come to the fore in recent years is the arrival of invasive plants and animals which have been brought to our country from overseas. The twelve most significant species at the moment are Japanese knotweed, Australian swamp stonecrop, giant hogweed, Himalayan balsam, water fern, floating pennywort, Chinese mitten crab, red-eared terrapin, mink, zander, American signal crayfish and zebra mussels. Less dramatic is the tendency of other plants such as Spanish bluebells to take over from our native species.

Fig 97. A view from the tower of All Saints church, Leamington Spa, looking over the Sydenham estate

Population Growth, Affordable Housing, Redundant Churches

The enlargement of the European Union to the east has led to large numbers of immigrants arriving in Britain in the first decade of the twenty-first century. Over one million new people arrived in the UK in the three years from 2003. This means that the population of Warwickshire has increased by approaching 7% from a figure which hovered around 500,000 for many years to an estimate of around 533,900 in 2005. Many of these people take employment which local people do not want but there is also likely to be higher unemployment of local people and pressure for more affordable housing. This will be exacerbated by

189

the credit crunch. Affordable housing is in short supply especially in the south of the county and in rural areas. House prices in 2007 were at such a level that family income needed to be three or four times the average wage in order for people to afford a basic two-bedroomed home by a conventional purchase route. Rents are unaffordable for many. Planning policies therefore advocate a stock of affordable homes which are subsidised and run by various forms of social housing providers. These are occupied either on a rental or shared ownership basis. We have already seen the pressure for market housing from people who find Warwickshire a desirable environment in which to live.

Birmingham	1,006,500
Solihull	205,600
Coventry	306,600
North Warwickshire	62,300
Nuneaton & Bedworth	120,700
Rugby	92,000
Stratford-on-Avon	116,100
Warwick	132,900

Fig 98. Population of Cities and Districts in Warwickshire (mid 2006 estimates)

The population of the whole of the West Midlands region was 5.18 million in 1982, becoming 5.37 million by mid 2006. The net migration into West Midlands in 2006 was much reduced at 13,000. The pressure for more houses on green land since is intense.

The result of all the changes we have seen over the centuries is that many villages have now turned into commuter dormitories. It seems that many people in Warwickshire want to live outside town but close enough to commute to work or to do the shopping. The fate of villages is an interesting study. First the indigenous population feels invaded by the incomers who retire to the village or live there to commute. As the population becomes less homogeneous there is the loss of the feel of a close community and it becomes easy to lose sight of the social needs of the community. Some newcomers to the village tend to adopt a 'drawbridge' attitude in which they see issues only from their own point of view. Rural Britain used to be a place where a few lords of the manor held sway over a largely peasant population but now this role is being taken over by the urban middle class.

One encouraging development is the existence of the Churches Conservation Trust which looks after historically valuable redundant churches including St John the Baptist, Avon Dassett, All Saints, Billesley, St Michael and All Angels, Brownsover, All Saints, Chadshunt and St Peter, Wolfhamcote.

Business Developments, Home Workers, Quarrying, Windfarms

The complex world of business of today has evolved from the now distant time when members of a small community became expert in one task or another and other residents turned to them to do a particular job into the global business environment of today. In Warwickshire we have seen a sharp decline in manufacturing and, fortunately, the growth of service industries. One advantage is that offices tend to be multi-storey and take less space for each employee than factories. On the other hand there has been a growth in warehousing to distribute imported goods and these are single storey and have a low employee ratio compared to the floor area of the building. Warwickshire has benefited in this evolution as people have seen the county as a good place to live and businesses have moved here. This growth in businesses and the number of people has consequences for the infrastructure of transport and community services ranging from shops and cinemas to schools and hospitals.

There has been speculation about the growth in businesses operating from home using computers such as online retailing. Statistics indicate that in England there were 2.3 million (9%) homeworkers in 1997, 2.6m (10%) in 2001 and 3.1m (11%) in 2005. From these totals there were 0.9m (4%) teleworkers in 1997, 1.5m (5%) in 2001, 2.4m (8%) in 2005. Predictably 2.1m (7%) of teleworkers could not work at home without a telephone and computer. Figures for the West Midlands follow the national trend. In 2007 60% of new businesses were started from home. There were 181,235 home based self employed people in West Midlands in 2006.

Despite the export of many manufacturing jobs some activities such as construction of buildings and roads continues and the materials which are required are often produced locally. There are a number of thriving quarries in the county including stone at Hartshill, gravel at Bodymoor Heath, sand at Bubbenhall and clay for cement at Stockton.

The wish to use renewable sources of energy has led to the construction of wind farms around the country, on-shore and off-shore. None of these have been erected in Warwickshire so far but this will probably not be so for ever. There is much debate about whether there are sufficient consistent winds to make windfarms viable in the county.

Roads, Railways, Airports

In the twenty-first century we have seen the completion of the Barford bypass, upgrading of the West Coast Main Line railway and struggles over the proposed extension and more intensive use of Coventry Airport at Baginton. Work has begun on the western bypass for Rugby.

A temporary terminal building was permitted to remain at Coventry airport but proposals to build a new terminal were turned down. The courts have rejected the appeals. Birmingham airport had floated the idea of a second runway but has settled for a proposal for an extension to the existing runway which will require diversion of the A45. This airport handled 9 million passengers in 2005. The M6 toll road opened in December 2003 but has not been as well used as it was hoped and tolls have been increased to balance the accounts.

Fig 99. A view across the M40 with Chesterton windmill on the horizon

Government Policy, Tiers of Policies,
New Frameworks, Sustainability

The pattern of development in the countryside in future will depend greatly on legislation on planning policies decided at European, national, regional and local level. The Labour government, which was first elected in 1997, has vacillated over its policies on land use planning. Mixed messages have been given about the protection to be given to the countryside and green belts in particular. When John Prescott was deputy prime minister planning was part of his department, the ODPM (Office of the Deputy Prime Minister). He was quite supportive of the environment and the countryside. In 2006 the wheel turned and a succession of reports raised concerns about shortage of housing based on rising house prices and the growing number of households. Household numbers were growing as birth-rates rose, life expectancy increased, household sizes became smaller and waves of immigrants arrived, particularly from eastern Europe. Policy is developing to require increased rates of house-building throughout the West Midlands. Most of the district councils are under pressure to allocate more land for house-building than was previously planned.

Since the Structure Plan for Warwickshire was extinguished in 2006 there are three tiers of planning policy documents. Central government publishes the Planning Policy Statements (PPS), the West Midlands has its own Regional Spatial Strategy and each city, borough or district has a Local Plan. Now that the Structure Plan for Warwickshire has passed into history the Coventry-Solihull-Warwickshire sub region has increased in importance but has yet to publish a Plan. Some parish councils have a fourth tier of policy in the shape of development plans for their villages which can be regarded as supplementary planning guidance if adopted by the district council.

Another innovation of the Labour government is the concept of Local Development Frameworks (LDFs) to replace the familiar regimes of Local Plans. There is some uncertainty at the time of writing about the form and content of the portfolio of documents which will make up a LDF. The basis of the LDF will be a core strategy and other policies will be written to add detail as necessary. Each LDF will be subjected to scrutiny by planning inspectors. All the Local Plans in Warwickshire had been updated and agreed by the end of 2007 and the councils will not be in the vanguard of those developing the first LDFs although all have started work on core strategies for them.

The planning system has refused to settle down in the new millennium. There has been long debate over the meaning of 'sustainability' and the consensus seems to be that it is right to give equal weight to economic, social and environmental aspects when considering proposals for development.

Balancing Act, Rural Development Policy, Planning System, Natural England

Planners and politicians who hold the strings have to a balance many conflicting calls on the finite amount of land in the county. As mentioned above the main over-arching aim must be to balance the social, economic and environmental factors which affect any proposal. There is the jargon of BPEOs (Best Practicable Environmental Options) and BPMs (Best Practicable Means). The role of planning in rural areas is a balance between conservation, agriculture, recreation and development. There is a continuously growing sense that the countryside is under threat from many directions. Conservation may be the final answer to retain some pockets of countryside for the people of the future to enjoy. However conservation can be seen as only a backstop solution to preserve in some way the rural fantasy or rural idyll which many people have in the backs of our minds.

Fig 100. Astley Castle being restored in 2009 after a devastating fire in 1978

A key planning document for the countryside is the national Planning Policy Statement 7 on Sustainable Development in Rural Areas published in 2004. This declares that it has 4 aims –

1. To raise the quality of life and the environment in rural areas,

2. To promote more sustainable patterns of development,

3. To promote the development of the English regions by improving their economic performance so that all are able to reach their full potential,

4. To promote sustainable, diverse and adaptable agriculture sectors.

The sting is clearly in the third aim which frequently conflicts with the other three objectives.

The planning system is still largely based on the necessity to apply for planning permission for significant development. There are exceptions mainly based on the idea of permitted development rights and for specific categories such as agricultural buildings. There is also a separate application regime for transport developments and for mineral working or quarrying. Changes to permitted development rights in 2008 exempted domestic extensions up to a specified size from the necessity to have planning permission. In 2009 government agreed to set up a new body to examine and grant permission for major infrastructure proposals. In 2000 the government took the impact of development on the environment seriously and required developers to include Environmental Impact Assessments with many planning applications.

In October 2006 English Nature, the landscape, access and recreation elements of the Countryside Agency and the environmental land management functions of the Rural Development Service came together to form Natural England. It is vital that this new organisation takes a firm grip on the natural environment including the Green Belts.

Sensitive Areas, Footpaths, Recreation

There are 38 designated environmentally sensitive areas in Britain, a total of 3,108,000 hectares. The extent of protected land now also includes nature reserves run by private trusts and country parks run by local authorities. More funding has been made available for conserving our heritage from the National Lottery. There has also been a movement to encourage and simplify the recreation of walking by identifying long distance footpaths.

One difficult issue to deal with is recreation within the countryside, especially the Green Belt. There is continual pressure for football pitches with clubhouses, horse riding with stables and illuminated exercise areas and golf courses which grow clubhouses, conference facilities and hotels. Also in the economics of the modern countryside visitors are seen as an 'alternative crop' which comes to farm shops and craft centres, visits exhibition farms and stays in bed and breakfast accommodation. This is fuelled by the 18 million people nationwide who regularly escape from towns and cities into the countryside.

It has been inevitable that as agriculture developed there has been a loss of variety of landscape and wildlife. An untidy 'natural' landscape is anathema to farmers and is regularly criticised as ineffective use of land. It is ironic that so-called 'unused' Green Belt land has been identified by some as suitable for removal from the Green Belt.

Campaigners battle hard to 'hold the line' and prevent extinction of species or their loss in British habitats. There are 60,000 species of wildlife in Britain out of about 2,000,000 in the world.

Climate Change, Some Numbers,

A major policy area which has neared the top of the agenda of every politician is Global Warming or Climate Change. Political opinion centres on the reduction of carbon release into the atmosphere mainly as carbon dioxide.

This concern points to reduced use of carbon fuels. The twin objects are to make buildings use less energy and to use renewable energy sources instead of fossil fuels. The impacts on development in Warwickshire are awaited. There is a small use of wind powered generators and solar thermal energy generation and a first step is probably for all buildings to be better insulated.

Fig 101. A spring-time view of Rowington church

196

Statistics

Management of anything including the countryside, the landscape and rural affairs is governed by the truism that 'you can only manage what you can measure'. There is now a wealth of statistics available. Some are very accurate whereas some, such as population at any given time or in the future, are less accurate estimates.

There are 487 Local Nature Reserves covering an area of 25,000 hectares.

There are 333 National Nature Reserves covering 199,000 hectares.

There are 10 National Parks extending to 1,373,000 hectares.

There are 104 Special Protected Areas covering 327,000 hectares.

There are about 60,000 species in Britain and up to 2,000,000 in the world.

11% of the land of England and Wales is in urban use.

There are over 9,000 conservation areas in England and 134 of them are in Warwickshire. There are 29 in Warwick district, 19 in Rugby, 1 in Nuneaton, 10 in North Warwickshire and 75 in Stratford. Some of these are within the urban areas but the majority cover parts of the rural villages.

The Forestry Commission has 11 large forest parks in England and Wales but manages just three woods in Warwickshire at Oversley Wood, Hay Wood and Arley Wood.

There are 41 Areas of Outstanding Natural Beauty in England and Wales covering 34,090 hectares and part of the Cotswolds AONB reaches into southern Warwickshire. The Cotswolds AONB covers 2,038 square kilometers.

In 1947 there were about 59 trees per acre in England but there are now only about 12.

Fig 102. Some statistics for England and Wales in 2008

Warwickshire Wildlife Trust has 50 reserves covering a total of 800 hectares (2,000 acres). Nature reserves run by Warwickshire Wildlife Trust cover parts of the county from Alvecote in the north to Tysoe in the south and from Earlswood in the west to Ashlawn Cutting by Rugby in the west.

Country parks in Warwickshire include – Alvecote Priory, Pooley Country Park and Heritage Centre, Kingsbury Water Park, Hartshill Hayes Country Park, Ryton Pools Country Park, Ufton Fields Nature Reserve, Burton Dassett Hills Country Park, the Stratford-upon-Avon Greenway and the Kenilworth to Berkswell Greenway.

There are 163 Grade 1 Listed Buildings in Warwickshire: Birmingham 21, Coventry 19, Nuneaton 3, Rugby 6, Solihull 12, Stratford 65 and Warwick 30.

Fig 103. Some statistics for Warwickshire in 2008

Amongst the species lost in the last hundred years are the fritillary, purple emperor butterfly, sand lizards and corncrake.

Growth or Stagnation, Final Thoughts

At the start of the century the Coventry-Solihull-Warwickshire Sub Regional Study identified the conflicting ambitions of the partners. All three major local authorities wanted to keep the Green Belt, Solihull wanted to become bigger in order to be economically viable, Coventry wanted to be bigger but was concerned that it had no scope to extend in any direction and Warwickshire wanted a bigger population. However there was an overall agreement with the Government to plan for growth in the West Midlands.

As this story ends we will look at a few more snippets from around the county.

A walk near Shuttington reveals a vista of spoil heaps to the south with open countryside to the north but there is a distant threat of open-cast mining. Alvecote lakes are an SSSI maintained by the Warwickshire Wildlife Trust. The Bird in Hand pub at Austrey is still thatched at the time of writing. The Four Counties pub at No Mans Heath is near the point where Warwickshire, Leicestershire, Derbyshire and Staffordshire meet and is an Asian restaurant in 2009. Purley quarry is beside the Mancetter lake which is a deep aquamarine colour derived from the ores in the soil. Easenhall has a striking lodge building alongside the cricket green. Haselor must have been an unruly place at some time in the past because there are stocks for three men and there is also a pillory at Coleshill. Stoneton Manor Farm near Priors Hardwick has a restored moat. The late medieval pattern of small irregular fields remains in the Arden area today with tree-lined hedges which give a familiar rural appearance. The once all-enveloping woodland has been reduced to sporadic patches and Arden is now mainly dairy with arable and fruit on more porous knolls. We have followed the life of a number of villages and end with the story of the size of Chesterton. It is now 3585 acres and the population has declined steadily since 1901 when it was 142. It rose to a peak of 287 in 1931 but dwindled away to just 100 in 1978.

Debate on the Future, Conflict, Sustainability, Balance

As we try to take a more or less dispassionate view of the future of the landscapes of Warwickshire at the start of the twenty-first century we find that the built-up area is expanding, the demand for building material is increasing, more roads are being built, the Green Belt is under pressure, farming is in flux and manufacturing industry has all but disappeared and service and distribution industries are replacing the jobs. Similar things are happening in many places all around the country but much of the countryside of Warwickshire in particular appears to be under intense pressure from developments. As this book goes to press the West Midlands region is considering housing targets until 2026.

Perhaps unfortunately for the countryside many of the Warwickshire landscapes are seen as desirable places in which to live. A number of attractive local towns provide much that the local consumers desire. Shopping at Coventry and Solihull is near the centre, there is easy transport to the large cities of Birmingham and London and there is high employment in service industries including catering.

There are distinct differences in the way in which parts of the county are developing. Stratford and Warwick Districts are honey-pots where market housing does not keep pace with demand because planning policies restrict the availability of land. There is a strong feeling that development must not be allowed to destroy what is attractive about the area. Considerable amounts of housing are built on sites created by demolition of sound houses with spacious gardens or, indeed, on the gardens themselves. This has become known as 'garden grabbing'. There is some sympathy for house builders who see a strong demand but are unable to find the land on which to meet that demand.

Rugby has expanded to the north with housing and warehousing in the large gap towards the M6 motorway. The future of the BT radio station site is uncertain as claims are made that the whole site is 'previously developed land' and therefore fair game for development. The spread of Rugby across the high plain seems irresistible.

Nuneaton and Bedworth are developing less quickly. This area still suffers from the decline in coal mining and the most deprived areas of the county are located in the borough. The landscape has the legacy of the extraction industries but is not under intense pressure for development although a number of trading estates and distribution depots have been developed in the gap between the two towns because of the proximity of the M6.

In North Warwickshire the countryside around Atherstone and Coleshill is also under less pressure from development than in the south. The developed areas of north Solihull press hard on the western boundary but the M42 provides something of a barrier for the moment. There is massive warehousing on the sites of Birch Coppice Colliery and Hams Hall.

There is a strong temptation to preserve the most attractive villages but they are places where people live and have ambitions to improve their properties. So the pressures for housing and commercial building are the major impact to be resisted in protecting the remaining countryside.

Tourism plays a large part in the economic life of the county, especially in the south. Stratford-upon-Avon remains a magnet as the refurbished Royal Shakespeare Theatre is being developed. Warwick Castle has over 800,000 visitors a year which is among the highest to any attraction in the country. Pressure to build and extend hotels in the countryside is unceasing.

Many of us have a rosy and romantic vision of country life in the past. In our mind's eye we think of cows grazing, skylarks ascending, fields of corn, corn-cockles, cornflowers, poppies, hedges and wildlife, swallows and shimmering streams. This is a distorted image which is an idealised view of a complex mixture of good and the bad elements. Even more so it does not represent the state of the countryside at this present time or what it is likely to become in future. We have to be clear what we want to preserve and what we want to conserve from what exists at the present. We also need to decide how to pay for conservation and preservation and, in particular, for retaining landscape features which are generally seen as desirable. It is necessary to take account of many organisations, or pressure groups, which each have a different view of what the future should be and how to achieve it. The Story Unfolds...

THE END

Appendix One

Acknowledgements

The writing of this work has entailed no original archaeological, agricultural, architectural or geological research on the ground by the author. I have relied entirely on studying existing printed and internet sources.

Fig 104. A view at Princethorpe. The orange object is an oil pipeline marker.

Many diverse areas of knowledge have been used in writing this book. It is the result of the collection of bits and pieces of information over a number of years. Sometimes the conclusions and opinions of authors conflict and this has been noted in the text. The vast army of local historians who write village histories have been of inestimable value. I am grateful to all the authors for their researches and writings and some of the most important ones are listed here. I acknowledge the hard and dedicated work of all those people who have dug deep into historical records of their villages and written up their research or who have devoted their lives to historical research and publication of it. I am grateful to Warwickshire Library for their resources.

Similarly the internet has been an almost limitless source of information. Of course many websites are not moderated and some infamous spoofs have been published on the web and it has therefore been plundered with caution. I have tried to double-check all references. Again I am grateful to the mainly anonymous creators of the websites which are listed.

The photographs and small drawings are by the author unless stated otherwise.

BOOKS

Alcester Local History Society, Alcester - A History
Aston, Michael, Interpreting The Landscape
Beckinsale, R & M, English Heartland
Blunden, John and Turner, Graham, Critical Countryside
Blunden, John and Curry, Nigel, Changing Countryside (The)
Bowers, John and Cheshire, Paul, Agriculture the Country and Land Use
Bragg, Melvyn, Travels in Written Britain
Carson, Rachel, Silent Spring
Cullingworth, B & Nadin, V, Town and Country Planning in the UK
Davis, Tony, Bedworth
Fairbrother, Nan, New Lives New Landscapes
Greed, Clara, Introducing Town Planning
Green, Bryn, Countryside Conservation
Hill, David, Atlas of Anglo Saxon England
Hill, Howard, Freedom to Roam
Hooke, Della, England's Landscapes - West Midlands
Hooke, Della, Warwickshire's Historical Landscape – The Arden
Hooke, Della, Morton Bagot
Hoskins, WG, Making of the English Landscape
Mabey, Richard, Common Ground (The)
McEwen, Malcolm, Future Landscapes
McGrory, David, Coventry
Martin, J M, Village Traders and the Emergence of a Proletariat in South Warwickshire, 1770 to 1850
Mercer, Derrik, Rural England
Newby, Howard, Countryside in Question
Newby, Howard, Green and Pleasant Land
Paturi, Felix, Nature, Mother of Invention, Distinction between development and design
Pye-Smith, Charles and Rose, Chris, Crisis and Conservation
Rackham, Oliver, History of the Countryside
Rainsberry, Edward, Long Compton - Through the Lych Gate
Roberts, B K, Colonization of Arden

ACKNOWLEDGEMENTS

Rolt, LTC, Worcestershire (Robert Hale)
Shoard, Marion, The Theft of the Countryside
Slater, Terry, History of Warwickshire
Slater and Jarvis , Field & Forest - a historical geography of Warwickshire and Worcestershire - 1982
Slater, TR and Bartley, G, Rural Settlements in Warwickshire
Smith, Graham, Warwickshire Airfields Second World War
Thomas, Lewis, Lives of a Cell
Tyack, Geoffrey, Warwickshire Country Houses
Wager, Sarah, Woods, Wolds and Grove
Warwickshire County Council and Countryside Commission, Warwickshire Landscape Guidelines c1990 – 3 volumes
West Midlands, Royal Town Planning Institute, Region and Renaissance - West Midlands, 1950 to 2000 – Brewin Books
Whitelock, Dorothy, The Anglo Saxon Chronicles, A Revised Translation
Yorke, Trevor, Tracing the History of Villages
Unknown, No Bricks Without Mortar - 50 years of A.C.Lloyd (Builders/Developers) 1948 to 1998
Unknown, Historical Atlas of Britain
Unknown, Kineton - the Village and its History
Unknown, Nuneaton - in the Making - Town Growth
Unknown, The Story of Coleshill
Unknown, Nature, Conservation and Farming

WEBSITES

Alcester, http://www.alcester.co.uk/History-29.asp
Ancient Monument Society, http://www.ancientmonumentssociety.org.uk/
Atherstone, http://www.atherstone.org.uk/
Atherstone, http://www.atherstonehistory.co.uk/
Bedworth Society, http://www.bedworth-society.co.uk/
Changing Landscape, http://www.thechanginglandscape.co.uk/change3.html
Country Quotes website, http://www.quotegarden.com/country.html
Enclosure, http://www.bahs.org.uk/15n1a2.pdf
Fortified England, www.fortifiedengland.co.uk
Geology, http://home.freeuk.net/webbuk2/geology.htm
Halls Around Nuneaton, http://www.webspinners.org.uk/weddingtoncastle2/new_page_40.htm
History of Roads, http://www.lancashire.gov.uk/environment/historichighways/roadplan/chapter2.asp?print=yes

Megalithic, http://www.megalithic.co.uk/
National Parks website, http://www.nationalparks.gov.uk/learningabout/history.htm
Pesticides History, http://www.pestmanagement.co.uk/lib/history
Planning on Wikipedia,
http://en.wikipedia.org/wiki/Town_and_country_planning_in_the_United_Kingdom
Quarrymans walk around Nuneaton, http://www.quarrymanswalk.co.uk/
Roman Britain, www.Roman-Britain.org
Short History of English Agriculture, Curtler, WHR - full text on web,
http://www.gutenberg.org/files/16594/16594-8.txt
Turnpikes website,
http://www.turnpikes.org.uk/English%20turnpike%20table.htm
Ullenhall history, http://ullenhall.net/?page_id=12
Warwickshire Time Trail, http://timetrail.warwickshire.gov.uk/
Warwickshire Archives, http://archivesunlocked.warwickshire.gov.uk/
Windows on Warwickshire web, http://www.windowsonwarwickshire.org.uk/
Warwickshire archaeology website, http://www.warwickshire.gov.uk/Web/corporate/pages.nsf/Links/2D30CFC51B4F01CF80256A25003097BB

Appendix Two

Walks

It is hoped that many readers will be prompted by this book to visit many of the landscapes mentioned. It is not possible to give detailed itineraries for a useful number of walks. The aim is to indicate here some sites where various features mentioned in the book can be seen from a gentle walk. It should be quite easy to plot a course for a walk using Ordnance Survey maps and many walking guides have been produced in print and on the internet which often include directions to a pub or teashop. Leaflets are often available from Tourist Information Centres. Please remember to keep to the public paths because, frustratingly, many interesting sites are on private land. Do ask for permission before going off the footpath.

Fig 105. A stroll on the Burton Dassett Hills

Please follow the Country Code published by Natural England –

- *Be safe, plan ahead and follow any signs.*
- *Leave gates and property as you find them.*

205

- *Protect plants and animals and take your litter home.*
- *Keep dogs under close control.*
- *Consider other people.*

A number of specific sites are listed but in the main these walks are an opportunity to enjoy the landscapes including the lie of the land, the geological features, the character of the rolling hills, the woods, the field patterns, the archaeological evidence and so on.

There are a number of long distance paths which pass through Warwickshire and leaflets are widely available from Tourist Information Centres and council offices. Much can be enjoyed by walking short lengths of these paths. They include:-

- **The Centenary Way** which runs within Warwickshire from Kingsbury to Meon Hill.
- **The Heart of England Way** which runs from Lichfield to Chipping Campden by way of Kingsbury, Berkswell, Henley in Arden and Bidford on Avon.
- **The Heart of Arden Way** which plots a circular course in the vicinity of Henley in Arden and Alcester.
- **The D'Arcy Dalton Way** which starts at Wormleighton and runs through to Wiltshire.
- **The Cotswolds Walk** which follows paths from Stratford upon Avon to Mickleton and on to Cheltenham.

A number of other walks starting and ending in Warwickshire towns and villages are listed below.

- **Alcester.** The town has a Roman history and a Roman museum and interesting buildings in Malt Mill Lane. There is a good walk through Wixford to see the local landscapes.
- **Atherstone-on-Stour.** This walk leads through the disused airfield where various defence relics can be seen including a control tower, two pillboxes, a battle headquarters, three air raid shelters, a shooting range and a hangar.
- **Austrey.** Highlights include ancient Salt Street, the Four Counties public house and the 'Gateway to Warwickshire' Bridge over the M42.
- **Chesterton.** This village has a chequered history. There is evidence of a deserted village, Roman history, the windmill, a water mill, the church and the M40.
- **Coleshill.** The Midland plain, Maxstoke Priory and Castle, Blythe Hall, Whitacre water works, Cole End Bridge.

- **Flecknoe.** Disused railway, canal and the deserted village of Wolfhamcote nearby.

- **Greenway, Stratford upon Avon.** This path follows the disused railway along the Avon Valley.

- **Moorwood Geological Trail.** This starts at Hartshill Hayes country park and signs indicate sand, shale, volcanic evidence, a quarry and geology in a disused railway cutting.

- **Napton.** The Oxford canal stop line can be seen with two pill boxes and anti tank blocks. There are the canal locks and the church and windmill on the top of the hill.

- **Polesworth.** A number of sites in the area including Abbey Green Park, Abbey church and gateway, Nethersole Centre, Bramcote Hall, canal, railway, Alvecote pools, Pooley Hall and Pooley Hall colliery.

- **Shustoke.** Daw Mill colliery, Shustoke Hall, Whitacre water works, Shustoke almshouses and Elizabethan fish ponds.

Appendix Three

Warwickshire Landscape Types

In the 1980s a project was begun to categorise all landscape types in England. One early project was undertaken jointly in Warwickshire by the Countryside Commission and Warwickshire County Council. The results were published in three sections in 1990. This was a detailed piece of work which divided the county into 25 areas which were carefully delineated on maps. There is a lot of intermingling and overlap of these areas and the most built up areas are excluded. It is a very complex report and it is not always easy to recognise in which area each place is positioned. This Appendix gives a brief overview of this work.

Fig 106. A view from Ilmington Hill

In this book we have generally used a simplified division of the county into three areas, Arden, Avon Valley and Feldon. However this more academic study identified seven major areas, Arden, Dunsmore, High Cross Plateau, Mease

208

Lowlands, Avon Valley, Feldon and Cotswolds. Most of these were then subdivided into smaller more specific types of landscape. The High Cross Plateau and the Mease Lowlands are small areas to the north-east of Arden. Dunsmore is part of Feldon and the Cotswolds adjoins the southern fringe of Feldon.

Arden

Ancient Arden. This covers two main areas. The first is the eastern part of the North Warwickshire plateau and the other is the belt of land from Hatton towards Redditch. The views are generally of small woodlands with small to medium fields. There are often typical sunken trackways and field ponds.

Arden Pastures. This is a rolling landscape with small fields and paddocks with mature trees in hedgerows including many oaks. There is some permanent pasture and narrow lanes with significant ribbon development.

Industrial Arden. This is a degraded landscape with closed mines and spoil-heaps. There are some small hedged fields. Terraced houses alongside lanes are typical.

Arden Parklands. A gently rolling landscape with wooded areas typically at the edge of estates associated with large country houses. There is some bracken with thick hedges.

Wooded Estate Lands. This is a large scale rolling landscape with hilltop woodlands. There are medium to large fields.

Arden River Valleys. This area includes the Rivers Arrow, Alne and Blythe and part of the Cole which meander through trees and meadows. There are elders and scrub with some pollarded willows.

River Valley Wetlands. A flat alluvial plain along the River Tame where there is considerable evidence of sand and gravel extraction.

Dunsmore

Plateau Farmlands. This is a gently rolling plain with an empty feel. There are farms and woodland with some remnants of heathland.

Plateau Fringe. Undulating land with some wooded river valleys. It is typified by large arable fields with isolated farms.

Dunsmore Parklands. An area of mainly parkland and estates with middle distance views enclosed within woodland edges.

High Cross Plateau

Open Plateau. Large wide views of rolling landscape. There are often scrappy hedges. It is lightly populated with isolated farms and manors.

Village Farmlands. A well defined pattern of hedged fields with some nucleated villages.

Mease Lowlands.

The north eastern tip of the county falls within this area along the River Mease. There are low hills with large fields with distinct hedges and some large country houses with estates attached.

Avon Valley

River Meadowlands. Flood meadows and some steep wooded bluffs. They are mainly grazing meadows with hedges following the valleys.

Terrace Farmlands. A fertile area which is on broad terraces. There is intensive farming with many greenhouses.

Vale Farmlands. This is a broad vale at the foot of the Cotswolds. There is a pattern of medium sized villages with straight roads.

Vale Orchard Belt. A large scale rolling landscape with many orchards. Prominent woods on hills and typical stone cottages.

Feldon

Ironstone Fringe. This is a large scale landscape with rolling hills. There is a feeling of isolation with some ironstone villages and wide roadside verges.

Vale Farmlands. Medium to large fields in a generally flat landscape with some isolated hills. There are a number of deserted villages.

Lias Village Farmlands. This is an undulating landscape with some wooded escarpments. There are small to medium fields and typical lias limestone buildings.

Feldon Parklands. Many large country houses in wooded estates.

Cotswolds

High Wold. This is a large scale rolling landscape with exposed hilltops and wooded valleys. There are some prehistoric barrows and stone circles.

The Wold. This is a rolling landscape with broad rounded hills which have some undeveloped land. The rich red soils are very productive.

Plateau Redlands and Edge Hill. There are large fertile arable fields of typical red soils. Small villages built of orange stone.

Cotswold Fringe. This northern end of the Cotswolds is a varied landscape of small rounded hills and valleys. Medium to large scale fields with small stone villages.

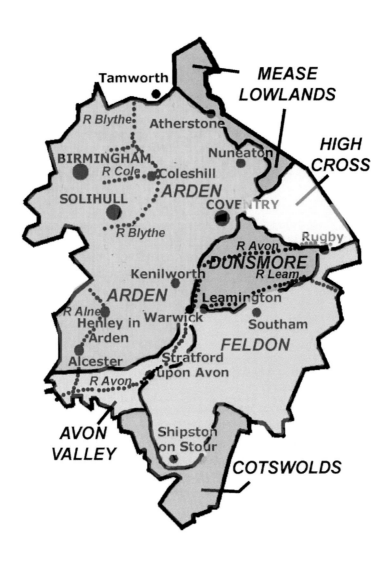

Fig 107. The major Landscape Areas identified in Warwickshire

Appendix Four

A Selection of Listed Buildings in Rural Warwickshire

This Appendix is a list of a selection of the Listed Buildings in Warwickshire. It is an idiosyncratic and personal list of favourites. It shows the range of what 'buildings' are listed and how widespread they are. It only includes buildings located outside the major towns. The buildings are Grade II unless stated otherwise.

North Warwickshire, 586 Listed Buildings including 7 Grade I, 53 Grade II*
Church of St James, Great Packington (Grade I)
Maxstoke Castle, Maxstoke (Grade I)
Stone House farmhouse, Fillongley (Grade II*)
Packington Hall (Grade II*)
Hartshill Grange, Hartshill (Grade II*)
Kingsbury Hall, Kingsbury (Grade II*)
Church of St Michael and All Angels and Churchyard Cross (Grade II*)
Priory Farmhouse, Church Road, Maxstoke (Grade II*)
Remains of Monastic Church, Maxstoke (Grade II*)
Merevale Abbey, Merevale (Grade II*)
Merevale Hall, Merevale (Grade II*)
Church of St John the Baptist, Middleton (Grade II*)
Middleton Hall, Middleton (Grade II*)
Botts Green Hall, Nether Whitacre (Grade II*)
Church of St Mary, Newton Regis (Grade II*)
Hoar Hall, Over Whitacre (Grade II*)
Pooley Hall, Polesworth (Grade II*)
Church of All Saints, Seckington (Grade II*)
Priory Farmhouse, Shustoke (Grade II*)

Shustoke Hall Farmhouse, Shustoke (Grade II*)
Church of St Chad, Wishaw (Grade II*)
Atherstone Lock No 5
Austrey Baptist Church
Cartshed, Dunton Hall, Curdworth
Curdworth Canal Tunnel
Canal Depot, Hartshill
The Bothie, Over Whitacre
Dovecote, Blyth Hall, Shustoke
Telephone Kiosk, The Green, Shustoke
Alvecote Priory, Shuttington

Fig 108. Arbury Hall was gothicised starting around 1750

Nuneaton & Bedworth, 94 Listed Buildings, 3 Grade I and 7 Grade II*
Arbury Hall (Grade I)
Chamberlaine's Almshouses, Bedworth (Grade II*)
Church of St Giles, Bedworth (Grade II*)
The Tea House, Arbury (Grade II*)
Park Farmhouse, Arbury Park (Grade II*)
South Farm, Arbury Park (Grade II*)
Water Tower, Bedworth

Solihull, 377 Listed Buildings including 12 Grade I and 39 Grade II*
Castle Bromwich Hall (Grade I)
Church of St John the Baptist, Berkswell (Grade I)
Grimshaw Hall, Solihull (Grade 1)
Knowle Hall, Balsall (Grade II*)
Templars Hall, Balsall (Grade II*)
Eastcote Hall, Barston (Grade II*)
Berkswell Hall, Berkswell (Grade II*)
Ram Hall, Berkswell (Grade II*)
Marston Hall, Bickenhill (Grade II*)
Diddington Farmhouse, Hampton-in-Arden (Grade II*)
Packhorse Bridge, Hampton in Arden (Grade II*)

Birmingham, 1468 Listed Buildings, 21 Grade I, 101 Grade II*
Aston Hall (Grade I)
New Hall, Sutton Coldfield (Grade I)
Blakesley Hall (Grade II*)
Sheldon Hall (Grade II*)
Kings Norton Guillotine Lock (Grade II*)
Metchley Abbey (Grade II*)
Highbury Hall (Grade II*)
Moor Hall Farmhouse (Grade II*)
Vesey Grange (Grade II*)
Water Orton Bridge (Grade II*)
Barns, New Shipton Farm (Grade II*)
Wake Green Road, Birmingham, prefabs

Coventry, 284 Listed Buildings, 19 Grade I, 21 Grade II*
Windmill Farmhouse, Birmingham Road
Pickford Farmhouse, Brick Hill Lane
Hazel Grove Farmhouse, Wall Hill Road
Cottages, Sutton Stop

Warwick, 1487 Listed Buildings, 30 Grade I, 85 Grade II*
Church of St Margaret and graves, Wolston (Grade I)
Baddesley Clinton House (Grade I)

Church of St Mary, Haseley (Grade I)
Kenilworth Castle (Grade I)
Abbey ruins, Kenilworth (Grade I)
Church of St Mary the Virgin, Lapworth (Grade I)
Packwood House (Grade I)
Stoneleigh Abbey (Grade I)
Warwick Castle (Grade I)
Old Vicarage, Hatton (Grade II*)
Offchurch Bury (Grade II*)
Pinley Abbey (Grade II*)
Yarningale Aqueduct (Grade II*)
Stare Bridge, Stoneleigh (Grade II*)
Abbey Ruins, Wroxall (Grade II*)

Rugby, 512 Listed Buildings, 10 Grade 1, 40 Grade II*
Combe Abbey, Combe Fields (Grade I)
Church of St Edith, Monks Kirby (Grade I)
Church of St Margaret, Wolston (Grade I)
Ansty Hall (Grade II*)
Church of St Botolph, Burton Hastings (Grade II*)
Tennis Court, Combe Abbey (Grade II*)
Princethorpe College (Grade II*)

Stratford-upon-Avon, 3343 Listed Buildings, 65 Grade I, 164 Grade II*
Town Hall, Alcester (Grade I)
Ragley Hall (Grade I)
Mary Arden's House, Aston Cantlow (Grade I)
Church of St Nicholas, Beaudesert (Grade I)
Bidford Bridge (Grade I)
Charlecote Park (Grade I)
Chesterton Windmill (Grade I)
Compton Verney (Grade I)
Ettington Park Hotel (Grade I)
Honington Hall (Grade I)
Church of St Nicholas, Loxley (Grade I)
Alscot Park (Grade I)
Church of St Peter, Wormleighton (Grade I)

INDEX

INDEX

221

INDEX